Michael O'He...

My Life and Times

Michael O'Hehir

My Life and Times

BLACKWATER PRESS

Editor

Deirdre Bowden

Design & Layout

Paula Byrne

ISBN

0 86121 604 0

British Library Cataloguing-in-Publication Data
A catalogue record for this book is available from the British Library
O'Hehir, Michael. Michael O'Hehir: My Life and Times.

Produced in Ireland by
Blackwater Press
c/o Folens Publishers
8 Broomhill Business Park
Tallaght
Dublin 24

Acknowledgements

The driving force behind this book is Michael himself. However, writing was always long-fingered for him due to his hectic work schedule. Since he suffered a stroke in 1985 the desire to put the details of his exciting career on record intensified and the seeds of this book were sown during his frequent visits to Eyeries on the Beara Peninsula in West Cork. There, while staying with his daughter Mary and family, his first recollections were recorded by Mary and her daughter Siúna.

Michael would like to acknowledge the invaluable assistance he has received from co-writers Maurice Quinn and Mick Dunne. He would also like to thank all those people who generously provided photos and other material for inclusion in this book.

Finally, thanks goes to John O'Connor, Deirdre Bowden and Anna O'Donovan at Blackwater Press, and Michael Croke and all the staff of RTE for seeing this book safely into production.

Contents

Foreword

Very few people enter the subconscious of a nation. Michael O'Hehir achieved this through his distinctive voice, telling the story of our national games and capturing the excitement of horse racing.

From his first radio broadcast while still a schoolboy he brought to his sports coverage on radio, and later on TV, a character of vibrancy which became part of the enjoyment of what he described. It was not just the game or the race which was recalled with pleasure, but how Michael had talked it through. He set the scene, conveyed the atmosphere, described the small details with an eye for what really mattered on the day, knew everyone by their name (and nickname), and filled in their background. He achieved the impossible: he made listening to radio a colour rather than a black and white experience!

Not surprisingly, Michael O'Hehir became a well-loved personality at GAA games and in racing circles, and among sportsmen and women. This affection for him was evident when he visited Áras an Uachtaráin with a number of hurling and camogie stars, on the occasion of the presentation of *The Hurling Giants* by Brendan Fullam, and he continues to be a welcome presence at Croke Park on the big days.

His skill and expertise as a sports commentator were recognised outside Ireland. Memories of the BBC coverage of the Aintree Grand National over a long period include Michael O'Hehir's voice, picking up the commentary at Becher's Brook and taking it on to the Canal Turn, a vital section of the race where many a favourite fell!

His outstanding talent for description and evoking atmosphere enabled him to respond to the unexpected task of covering in the United States the assassination of President John F. Kennedy and later his funeral. His coverage of this tragic international event showed his qualities as a truly great broadcaster.

Illness, alas, has brought his career prematurely to a close but his story will be widely welcomed.

Mary Robinson

UACHTARÁN NA HÉIREANN
PRESIDENT OF IRELAND

1

In School Cap and Blazer — The Early Years

In May of 1938 I was studying for the Leaving Certificate examination — or should have been. But on a particular morning in May, as I cycled to school in O'Connell CBS from our home in Drumcondra, subjects like Irish, English, Maths or any of the others on that year's course were not, I can assure you, dominating my thoughts. I was preoccupied with finding a telephone box to make what would turn out to be one of the most — if not the most — important phone calls of my life.

Call it bumptiousness, brazenness or anything you wish, but I was intent on telephoning a certain Dr T.J. Kiernan, who just happened to be the Director of Broadcasting in Radio Éireann, no less. Stepping into the kiosk, here I was a cocky schoolboy still not 18 for another few weeks, ringing the radio station and asking to be put through to the Director, if you don't mind. That was me, full of confidence that I could become a sports commentator even as a schoolboy. As luck would have it I was connected with Dr Kiernan and there, you could say, began a career that would have my name integrally linked with hurling and Gaelic football, and later racing, for the next 40 years or so.

You see, a few weeks before I had written to Dr Kiernan asking for a test as a commentator. At that time Radio Éireann had no regular commentator for Gaelic Games and they used different people. Indeed, the year before, the station had a dispute with the GAA over the choice of commentators for the Railway Cup finals with the result that the matches on St Patrick's Day were not broadcast. But, even worse, when the 1937 All-Ireland hurling final between Tipperary and Kilkenny came around in September the row had not been resolved and there was no commentary. Instead the listeners got reports of the two halves which were broadcast by Sean Ó Ceallacháin [Senior] and Eamonn Barry from the Killarney post office. Happily the dispute was resolved by the time of the football final three weeks later and that game (Kerry v Cavan) was broadcast by one Father Michael Hamilton, then chairman of the Clare County Board but someone destined to be become much more prominent in the GAA in later years.

With youthful conviction I believed that I could do at least as well as any of those already doing the job when I wrote to Dr Kiernan. My parents looked on their 17-year-old's crazy notion with tolerant amusement, but they were amazed when I got a reply on the Friday of that week asking me to report to Croke Park on the following Sunday (16 May) to do a test during a football match between Louth and Wexford, a National League group final. I honestly knew nothing about the tests to be held and I turned up wearing my school cap, school blazer and grey flannels to find that I was one of five people being auditioned. Each of us was asked to do five minutes of the first half. Then at half-time word came through from Dr Kiernan's office in the GPO that the man — the man, mark you — who did the last five minutes was to do the second half. Well, I was 'the man' who did the second half and that was that. I went off about my business and back to school the following day.

A week passed, then a fortnight and I had heard nothing, so one morning I got off my bicycle on my way to O'Connell School, found that telephone and got through to the Director of Radio Éireann. I asked him about the tests and he said: 'Oh, the very man. I was just going to write to you. I wonder could you get time off work for a little while tomorrow and come in and we'll have a chat.'

Get off work! I was still in O'Connells, so I 'mitched' from school, went to the GPO and sat waiting to see Dr Kiernan, all the time wondering if he would say 'too young' when he saw me. I was barely 18 and looked an awful lot younger. Anyway I went in, he looked up, smiled and said 'would you sit down.' Then he started talking about the test and suggested I should give the scores more often. In a daze I heard him ask: 'Would you do the Leinster football final?' Would I what! It was beyond my wildest dreams and full of excitement I headed off to Clare for the school holidays. I spent much of my time over the next few weeks on my bike rehearsing aloud for the big day, much to the amusement of passers-by. As it turned out I had more time to practise than I thought as I received a letter, forwarded from Dublin, telling me that the Leinster final broadcast was cancelled and my first commentary was to be the All-Ireland semi-final on 14 August in Mullingar between Monaghan and Galway.

In those days, Radio Éireann didn't broadcast matches every Sunday during the summer. There was no lesser match for me to start on than the All-Ireland semi-final, so I was pitched in at the deep end, you could say. By way of preparation I wanted to get a good look at Monaghan (and Armagh), so I travelled with my friends and neighbours, the Kerrs, to see the Ulster final where Monaghan beat Armagh in a tough game.

You could say that broadcasting was still in its infancy in those late Thirties; certainly nothing like we know nowadays and we didn't even call it radio. Radio Éireann or 2RN, as the station sending out programmes on the wireless was then called, claimed to have broadcast the first live commentary on a sporting event in Europe. This was from the All-Ireland hurling semi-final between Kilkenny and Galway in August 1926 with the commentator P.D. Mehigan, who authored many, many books on the games as *Carbery* and was 'Pato' in *The Irish Times*. Maurice Gorham, once a Director of Broadcasting, in his *Forty Years Of Irish Broadcasting* says this claim was justified because 'the BBC was barred from doing commentaries by its obligation not to broadcast news before 7 p.m.' However, in America they had already been broadcasting sports events and it appears that the first live outside broadcast there in sport was in April 1921 of a boxing event by a station in Pittsburgh.

By 1938 sports commentaries were not commonplace or anything like as frequent as they now are. Therefore there was no question of set styles or standards. But I did get some valuable advice at the beginning from a BBC commentator of the time, Tommy Woodruff. A friend of mine, Monsignor Richard Glennon, suggested that I write to Tommy, whose brother, Father Woodruff, a Jesuit, was editor of *The Tablet*. I told Tommy what I was setting out to do and he was very helpful. We kept in contact until his death.

Why, you might well ask, sports broadcasting? The reply is that two things in my youth were responsible for setting the course of my life: being brought up in what could be called a GAA house and my passionate interest, from an early age, in wireless.

3

I was born in Dublin on 2 June 1920 of Clare parents. My father, Jim, came from Paradise and my mother, Esther Sheehan, from Newmarket, but she left Clare when still a baby and was brought up in Tullamore. They married in 1919 and we lived for a time at 29 Leeson Street in Dublin before moving to Ormond Road, just around the corner from the front gate of All Hallows College, in Drumcondra. Schooling began with the nuns at Holy Faith Convent, Glasnevin, St Patrick's National School in Drumcondra before moving to O'Connell School and the Christian Brothers on the North Circular Road. It would have been impossible to escape Gaelic Games in the Hehir household because if there is such a thing as a person being immersed in Gaelic Games then it was Jim Hehir. (My name, by the way, was Hehir until I spent three summers in the Carrigaholt Gaeltacht when I became Micheal Ó hÉithir and was introduced that way on radio for many years until the change to Michael O'Hehir came about when I joined the *Irish Independent* in 1944.)

My father worked in the Department of Local Government and had a lifelong, consuming interest in Gaelic Games. He was, at various times, attached to the Civil Service and Crokes clubs, but in 1942 he was invited to join the still-young St Vincent's by Father William Fitzpatrick, the man affectionately known as 'Dr Fitz' on Dublin's northside and co-founder with Brother Ernest Fitzgerald ten years earlier of the club that was to become nationally famous. Around that time, my Dad was taking things easy after many years serving on the Dublin County Board, but — as the official history of St Vincent's records — 'little did he know that his sojourn of tranquillity was to be so abruptly ended.' Jim Hehir went straight onto the executive committee and the following year he took over as the club chairman — a position he filled until 1949, a period during which the club prospered and expanded tremendously and during this time it was decided to restrict membership to those who were 'eligible to play in the minor grades or who were born in Dublin or who on the date of application were ordinarily resident in the parishes of Marino, Fairview, Clontarf.' This new policy was to have repercussions on the Dublin county football team within a few years. Most of the committee, like my Clare-born father, were from the country and it has been recorded that the St Vincent members 'of non-Dublin origin have been amongst the strongest defenders and vigilant watchdogs of its singular identity.'

At national level my dad's proudest moment was in 1914 when he trained the Clare hurling team to win the county's first All-Ireland championship. That team contained celebrated players like Pat 'Fowler' McInerney, Brendan Considine, Colonel Tom McGrath, Ambrose Power and Jack Shalloo. They trained in Lahinch and Quin for the Munster semi-final against Limerick and went on to beat Cork in the Munster final in Thurles. Then they beat Laois in the All-Ireland final on 18 October.

Years later my father turned to football — or rather Leitrim turned to Jim Hehir for help in 1927 when they won the Connacht championship for the first time and faced Kerry in the All-Ireland semi-final in Tuam. It seems there was a Leitrim friend of my father's working with him in the Civil Service who persuaded him to take over the training of that football team.

With my father so keen on the games it was nothing to be taken to four or five matches in Dublin on the same Sunday when I was growing up and, after a while, I played in some of them. Although I played a fair amount of hurling, I never played a football game in my life.

Being an only child I had to make my own amusement and, from an early age, I was fascinated with one of the new wonders of the modern world: the wireless. Like many other radio 'hams' I spent long hours fiddling with the dial trying to pick up foreign stations. I remember particularly tuning-in to *The Breakfast Show* from America. Spurred on by the inquisitiveness of youth, I learned how to take wireless sets apart and put them together again, but the parts I needed were not always readily available in Dublin. On one occasion I took an excursion train going to Belfast for a rugby international at Ravenhill with the sole purpose of buying a particular piece of equipment which I then smuggled home hidden in my overcoat. So it's hardly any wonder that radio and sport have dominated my life.

At last the great day for my first commentary arrived and I set off with my father by train for Mullingar, the venue of the Galway-Monaghan semi-final. I was nervous, I was anxious. I had done an awful lot of homework. Even so I felt I needed to make one more check on the players, so I called to the teams' hotels before they left for the ground.

At Cusack Park we climbed into a broadcasting box that had just enough room for myself and my father. He struck me as being in an even more nervous state than I was. Some 30 or 40 yards away in a kind of watchman's hut was Jimmy Mahon, the Radio Éireann technician. Through the headphones I got the word from Jimmy 'Two minutes to go ... one minute to go.' And then: 'You're on the air' and off I went. I tried to describe as best I could what was happening on the field. Many years later I was asked what I recalled from that first match and I honestly replied: 'I can't recall the score or even if it was a good match, only that Galway were a very good team.' The records show that Galway won 2-10 to 2-3 and it was reported as having developed into a one-sided game after the second quarter had promised a thriller. Monaghan that day didn't wear the white with the blue collars and cuffs that we see them in these days: instead they wore a black jersey with gold shoulders. Galway, of course, were in that brilliant maroon and white they had introduced about four years earlier.

During a lull in the game I mentioned that one of the linesmen was Joe Keohane, the Kerry full-back who would be playing in the other semi-final the following Sunday. It was the natural thing to say 'and there doing the line is the Kerry full-back, keeping a close eye on some of the players he might be coming up against: his name, of course, Joe Keohane.' But how was I to know that Joe was on sick leave from the Civil Service and had sent in a medical certificate — which had expired the previous week — saying that he was practically at death's door? For many years afterwards Joe, ever the rogue, claimed I nearly got him sacked! Another thing I remember about that day in Mullingar was a note being passed up to me from Jimmy Mahon, the technician, saying 'keep it up, going great,' at half-time. That was very much appreciated as was the drink offered to me by a total stranger. In those days there was no question of handing back to the studio at half-time so the time had to be filled. I decided to let the band play away and as I stepped out of the commentary box for a few minutes I was met by a man rushing up the steps, bottle in hand, bringing a drink for the 'poor lad' who was doing all the talking.

When it was all over and my father and I headed home not much was said because I was still not too sure how the whole thing had gone. The mood remained somewhat sombre until we got off the tram on Drumcondra Road and were met by Tommy O'Reilly, a family friend who became my right-hand man in later years. His reaction convinced me that it had gone well. With him was a reporter from the *Irish Independent* who had been sent out to do a story on this newcomer to the broadcasting world. I received an encouraging note from Dr Kiernan, and an engagement for the second semi-final, which was in Croke Park between Kerry and Laois the following Sunday. A cheque for £3 was also enclosed — expenses weren't even mentioned in those days!

That second semi-final was easier and I approached it with a good deal more confidence. That was the day the original Cusack Stand was officially opened. Then, my broadcasting career took a short break. I watched that year's All-Ireland hurling final from the old Hogan Stand with my friend, Monsignor Richard Glennon, while Dave Hanley, a schoolteacher and a prime mover in the Dublin Primary Schools' Leagues, did the commentary.

Consequently, I made my All-Ireland final debut at the 1938 football final, which provided us with lots of drama and excitement. It needed a draw and replay between Galway and Kerry. The first match attracted a huge crowd of 68,950, which was a new attendance record. It was real, traditional stuff; hard, honest-to-God football. For the replay the crowd, as often happens, was smaller (only just over 47,000) and like so many replays down the years it didn't have the quality of the drawn game. With ten minutes to go the Sam Maguire Cup was on its way to Galway. They were leading 2-4 to 0-7. Peter Waters, the referee from Kildare, blew the whistle for a free and, suddenly the crowd began to stream onto the field. They thought game was over.

Kerry also, it seems, mistook it for the final whistle and their players disappeared to the dressing-room and, it was said, that some of them even left Croke Park. Now if they did it must have been the quickest 'evacuation' in the history of that particular ground. However, when the game was restarted — and it was a case of playing only for a few minutes — there were six or seven Kerrymen out there who hadn't been on the original team among them Joe Keohane and

Murt Kelly, who had had a disagreement with the Kerry County Board and had asked not to be considered for the replay.

Years afterwards Joe told me: 'I actually paid my way into Croke Park that day. Towards the end of the game when the crowd thought it was over there was a lot of commotion and I don't think anybody was ever quite sure what the commotion was about. I was asked to go in and tog-out as a sub and I had to borrow togs, but I went out and played the few minutes that were left.'

One of the terrors of commentating is the feeling that you are talking to thousands and thousands of people. So in my early years in broadcasting I would picture in my mind's eye a place down in Clare called Ballycorrig and, up on a hill there, a man called Patrick Garry, who used to go to matches all over the country. For some years before I started broadcasting, he had been bedridden. So I'd imagine myself talking directly to him: this helped get rid of the feeling that I was addressing a multitude. In those formative years it was not the people of Ireland or anywhere I was speaking to, but to Patrick Garry, doing my best to tell him what was happening. That way I seemed to develop a style the radio audience seemed to like.

Funny thing is that after my first broadcast in Mullingar it took me about 25 years to catch up with Monaghan again. When I did commentate again on one of their matches in the early 1960s that left only one county that I never commentated on — Fermanagh. But in the mid-1960s I did a Fermanagh match completing the 32 counties for me.

2

War, Rationing, but Big Crowds

My first commentary on an All-Ireland hurling final was on the first Sunday of September 1939 — and I remember it well. But in the unlikely event that I might ever forget such a major milestone in my broadcasting career the Good Lord and the hurlers of Kilkenny and Cork combined to ensure that the occasion would be indelibly etched on my memory. This was the day of the 'Thunder and Lightning' final.

September 3, 1939. It was also the day that World War II began. However, as I recall it, the 39,000 and more of us heading for Croke Park that day were not truly conscious of the enormity of the news that broke at 11 o'clock that morning. Most assuredly none of us would then have anticipated the dreadful consequences of the announcement for the whole world — even for those of us here in neutral Ireland. There had been ominous signs and dark foreboding in the preceding weeks as Britain and France strove to contain Hitler's aggressive ambitions for Nazi Germany.

Two days before the threat of war had increased dangerously when Hitler's invading forces stormed into Poland. I remember being in a car that day with Paddy O'Keefe, the general secretary of the GAA, driving down Belvedere Place. We saw a character I knew as a racecard seller, a colours' seller and newsboy called Jockser coming up the street with his bundle of evening papers and shouting 'Stop Press' and carrying a poster which had just one word: WAR. One simple little word, telling us that the world was entering an era of death and devastation and deprivation we just could not envisage then. To be honest all the people going to Croke Park who would have heard of that morning's declaration of war were probably more immediately interested in Cork and Kilkenny.

That final was Cork's first since 1931, which meant an eight-year absence from the final unprecedented in the county's history up to then. It remained an unwanted record for Cork until they had that extraordinary gap of nine years when they failed to reach the finals from 1957 to 1965. It was also the first meeting of Kilkenny and Cork since the 1931 decider needed two replays to give Cork the championship. Consequently there was particular interest in the clash and the reality is that the impending doom in Europe took second place that weekend in the thoughts of devoted hurling supporters.

It had rained during the morning and it was still coming down as most of the people made their way to the ground, but the sun came out during the course of the afternoon. For the first 40 minutes of the match it was a glorious day, but we could see the clouds gathering. About ten minutes from the end there was a huge clap of thunder — bang, wallop — along with ferocious lightning. I remember seeing a flash of lightning going dancing across a wire that held the one microphone in the little wooden commentary box in Croke Park and it was really frightening. Talking once about that day Jack Lynch, one of the Cork stars of that era, remembered: 'It was a raging storm and the rain came down like stair-rods. During some bouts of the play it was very hard to see more than 20 yards away from you. The rain came down so heavily that the ground wasn't able to absorb it. The ground conditions were very difficult: it was almost unplayable.'

Despite the awful conditions it was a great game. Kilkenny led by six points at half-time but they had to withstand a determined Cork rally which brought an equalising goal with two minutes left.

Then disaster struck Cork. Kilkenny were awarded a '70' and when the ball came in it got to Jimmy Kelly — some people believed that a Cork back knocked it out with a fluffed clearance to the Kilkennyman — who scored the winning point. However I thought then, and I still believe, that the ball for that '70' was placed on the Kilkenny 70-yard line instead of the Cork 70-line, which would have meant it was about 15 yards further out from the Cork goal. With the torrential rain that battered the pitch it wasn't easy to see any lines and in the confusion of the appalling weather I believe the '70' was taken from the wrong line. So it fell short to Jimmy Kelly who got the winner.

* * *

As the war gathered momentum throughout Europe, and subsequently in the Pacific, Ireland was affected by shortages everywhere. As the late Pádraig Puirséal recorded in his *The GAA and Its Time* history 'by 1941 everyone had begun to feel the effects of "the Emergency". Coal was in short supply, trains ran at erratic speeds and to unpredictable time-tables — and often did not run at all.' Petrol was becoming scarce and travel increasingly restricted. People were getting out tandems and bicycles, even going to matches in pony-and-traps. What was known as the 'ghost train' from Kerry— it travelled through the night before any All-Ireland finals that Kerry were in — was, one year, the only train from Kerry. In 1944, for example, when Roscommon and Kerry met in the final the late PF (the well-known Kerry journalist, Paddy Foley) wrote in his *Kerry's Football Story*: 'only one train left Roscommon; there was only 'the ghost train' from Kerry, instead of the customary six specials of other years.' The same the previous year when Roscommon made their first appearance in the All-Ireland final — this time against Cavan — only one train was available from Roscommon. The county's great captain, Jimmy Murray, recalled: 'To get a ticket for that train was like getting a ticket for a match nowadays.' And yet there were some gigantic crowds even with the problems of travelling. I think, the fact that there were such big crowds in such difficult times was the best tribute anybody could pay to the popularity of the games all over the country.

It was amazing to be outside Croke Park on a big match day, especially in the mid-1940s. There were no cars, no taxis, but hundreds and hundreds of bicycles; no motor-bikes because people couldn't get the petrol for them, and scores of tandems. Lots of people literally came in tandem on tandems to see their stars in action. As historian Marcus de Burca wrote: 'At major stadia parking attendants now collected more in tips from cyclists than they had ever obtained from motorists.' Many of these people who came by these modes of travel had left their homes two and three days before matches so they wouldn't wind up exhausted; people lined up in the streets outside Croke Park, some sleeping through the night, on the eve of the All-Ireland finals waiting for the gates to open. This at a time when there was no such thing as all-ticket matches and when travel facilities were non-existent. On 1 May 1942 all petrol supplies for private cars were withdrawn and Sunday bus services were cancelled because of the fuel shortages. The situation was now so bad that the Central Council decided to abandon the junior and minor championships while the 'Emergency' lasted.

Needless to say attendances, in some cases, were badly hit, but in some instances this was a result of not very attractive pairings or what the public perceived to be unattractive draws. This was particularly so in hurling when Cork dominated and established their four-in-a-row record from 1941 to 1944. In 1940 there was a crowd of 49,260 at the Limerick-Kilkenny final, but a drop to 26,150 the following year when Dublin took on Cork. Even though Cork won by 20 points the attendance was up by over 1,000 when the same counties met again in 1942. Then the figures went up to nearly 49,000 in 1943 — at the worst period of fuel shortages and food rationing — when Antrim created a huge surprise by shocking Kilkenny and qualifying to meet Cork in the final. It was 26,000 again a year later for Cork v Dublin. Revenue for the GAA was reduced somewhat in those War years, but Marcus de Burca recorded an extraordinary feature of those times: 'What is surprising is that never during World War II did it [GAA] incur a loss on any year's operations, no matter how curtailed these were.' Probably one of the reasons for this is the fact that, although attendances dropped for hurling finals, there were some huge crowds at football games. Particularly when newcomers to the All-Ireland scene, Roscommon, came along.

For the Kerry-Galway final of 1940 there were 60,824 in Croke Park, but there was a drop for the next two years which may have been explained by Kerry being the hot favourites for the 1941 repeat with Galway and the appearance of Dublin in the 1942 decider. That was when Dublin teams included players who were natives of several counties and the sides did not have anything like the huge following the Dubs enjoy nowadays.

Then Roscommon arrived on the stage. Although they had won the junior championship in 1940 not many were expecting them to burst on the scene the way they did in the mid-1940s. At the time teams engaged in collective training. The players would come together, having withdrawn from their jobs on holidays, and be housed in a base for two or three weeks before the final, and sometimes the semi-final. It could be in a school, a hotel or, as happened in Roscommon's case, in one person's home. Dan O'Rourke, a teacher in Tarmon, had a lifelong association with Gaelic Games. He had played football for Roscommon and served as county chairman as well as a Fianna Fáil TD. He was responsible for a big upsurge in football in the county in the 1930s and a lot of the credit must go to him for taking Roscommon into prominence in the 1940s. He took the team into his home in Tarmon, had his garage converted into a dormitory; and not only housed the players but fed them three meals a day in his own house. Kerry, on the other hand, would usually be housed in St Brendan's College in Killarney for their semi-final training and would go through two sessions a day under the great Dr Eamonn O'Sullivan, usually indoor coaching in mid-morning and then the outdoor training and football that evening in Fitzgerald Stadium. For the All-Ireland finals, which were on the fourth Sunday of September in those years, the college (or 'the Sem' as it was called) would have the students back at school so Kerry usually stayed at a hotel. All teams, especially those with players scattered throughout the country, did the same.

However, by the mid-1950s certain people in the association were having doubts about this type of full-time training on the grounds that it was inconsistent with the amateur status of the organisation. So it was prohibited at the 1954 Congress after a special committee had carried out an investigation into the matter. We often hear people nowadays say that the players have been so much fitter in recent times than they were in those earlier years. But in those days of the collective training players got together for just a few weeks, they didn't spend their time sitting around playing cards; they got themselves very fit. Perhaps, it was a different game as far as the football was concerned, but those were very fit men by any standards.

Roscommon certainly benefitted from the full-time training. They qualified for the All-Ireland semi-final in 1943 and beat Louth to get to their first final. This caused tremendous interest and, in spite of the travel restrictions, so many supporters managed to get to Croke Park that the attendance was 68,023. It ended in a draw against Cavan and over 47,000 turned up for the replay on the second Sunday of October.

A year later Roscommon were back to defend their title and even some of their own followers were a little anxious because, having avoided Kerry the previous year, they now found themselves up against the mighty Kingdom. A massive 79,245 were there to smash the attendance records by more than 10,000. Roscommon were very conscious of the great fielding abilities of the Kerry backs and it was decided that they would play the ball low to their forwards. This tactic paid-off with the skill of men like Donal Keenan, later to become president of the association, Jimmy Murray, John Joe Nerney and Frankie Kinlough. May 1945 brought the end of the war in Europe and hostilities in the Pacific stopped in September, but it was a while before Ireland got back to normal as the scarcities continued. If that wasn't bad enough the summer of that year proved to be one of the wettest on record and from July onwards there was incessant rain which caused a succession of cancellations creating chaos with the championships. The All-Ireland semi-finals were played on schedule, Kerry beating Antrim (and surviving an objection by the Ulster champions) and Roscommon getting over Laois. The hurling final was played as expected on the first Sunday of September and Cork beat Kilkenny by nine points to complete a record sequence of six All-Ireland medals in succession for Jack Lynch. He had won four-in-a-row with the hurlers, then a football medal in 1945 when Cork beat Cavan in the final and now his sixth — a feat never since equalled.

By then people were becoming very worried about the effects of the bad weather on the harvest and the government called for volunteers to help the farmers gather in the crops, so many fixtures were called off. The football final between Kerry and Roscommon was postponed and when the rain eased it was staged on the first Sunday of October. Nearly 76,000 were at the game and they saw Kerry fall behind by seven points by the half-time break. Roscommon appeared to be coasting and were ahead by six points with about five minutes to go, but they were caught when Kerry's full-forward, Paddy Burke, scored two goals. Even the strongest of Kerry supporters would have admitted that Roscommon should have won that game. Having had it sewn up they seemed to throw it away in the last few minutes. Jimmy Murray, their captain who had gone off with an injury, admitted years afterwards that he was beginning to compose his victory speech on the sideline.

The replay was on 27 October and it was a classic. Kerry's great record in replays was being put to the test — they had won four All-Irelands in replays and the 1938 defeat by Galway was the only losing replay for them. In semi-finals and Munster finals they were then almost invincible. Now Roscommon led them by two points at half-time of this replay, but Kerry brought on their captain, Gus Cremin, whom they had surprisingly dropped for the final, and he made a big difference in the last quarter. He scored a very important point before a Gega O'Connor centre was bundled into the Roscommon net from a goalmouth mêlée for Kerry to win by four points. That marvellous match was seen by 65,661, but I still say Roscommon should have won it the first day.

One of the strangest occurrences of the wartime period happened in 1941. As mentioned, there was rationing and scarcity, but worse still in some parts of the country there was a very serious outbreak of foot and mouth disease, particularly in Munster and South Leinster, which lasted from about February until nearly October. The championships began but Tipperary and Kilkenny were two counties very badly hit by the scourge. They were due to meet Cork and Dublin in their respective provincial championships but the Department of Agriculture had restricted travel in the affected areas and Tipperary and Kilkenny weren't allow to travel.

Attempts were made to sort out the fixtures programme by swopping the dates of the All-Ireland finals: by playing the hurling on 28 September and the football on the first Sunday. But the Central Council resisted a request to have the hurling final delayed further and ruled that Munster and Leinster must nominate two counties to represent them in the final. To avoid later objections, the Council also ruled that if one of the nominated teams won the All-Ireland final it would get the championship. Cork were due to play Tipperary in Munster but were nominated to play Limerick on 14 September and they won easily. Dublin got the nomination from their provincial council and they beat Galway in the All-Ireland semi-final to put two nominated teams into the final. Cork won that even more comfortably 5-11 to 0-6 and were the All-Ireland champions — the first of their four consecutive titles. Tipperary and Kilkenny still hadn't been beaten in the championship, though, and when travel restrictions were eased in the middle of October arrangements were made for the two provincial finals.

Cork and Tipperary met in Limerick on 26 October and, sensationally, the new All-Ireland champions were beaten by Tipp by eight points. Consequently Cork are in the record books as that year's All-Ireland champions, but Tipperary as the Munster title-holders. In Leinster the Council was saved any blushes when Dublin beat Kilkenny at Croke Park by 2-8 to 1-8 on 2 November.

3

Give Me Five Minutes More...

As I left the commentary box at Croke Park on the last Sunday evening of October 1946 still filled with the thrills and tension of the classic replay between Kerry and Roscommon little did I think that the next All-Ireland football final I would see would be over 3,000 miles away. But that's what happened in September 1947 when the final was staged at the Polo Grounds in New York — a historic and unique occurrence because this was the only All-Ireland senior final (in hurling or football) to be played outside Ireland before or since. Looking back on it now we cannot fully appreciate what a massive undertaking it was at a time when commercial and civil trans-Atlantic travel, particularly by air, was still recovering from complete disruption during the war.

Members of younger generations, who nowadays take speedy jet travel and satellite sports broadcasting for granted, can have no real idea of what a daunting — even risky, certainly unheard of — venture it was to take the All-Ireland football final to America. When the proposal was first made not many people here at home took it seriously and, as time went on and the GAA was faced with making a final decision, not everyone approved of transporting the biggest event in the Irish sporting calendar across the Atlantic.

Where the idea originally came from is now clouded by the passage of time, but it appears that it originated in correspondence between John 'Kerry' O'Donnell, who was even then a very prominent official in the New York GAA, and Michael Canon Hamilton, later Monsignor, who was parish priest in Newmarket-on-Fergus and a long-time friend of the New York branch of the organisation. At the time, Gaelic games were at a low ebb all across America in cities where they had flourished for many decades, especially in New York which then as now had the strongest unit. The absence of so many young Irish and Irish-Americans who were serving in the US Forces combined with the complete ban on immigration from Ireland brought activity in hurling and football to a standstill in several cities and caused a serious fall-off in New York. Consequently Canon Hamilton, with encouragement from O'Donnell, made the case that bringing the football final to New York would be a tremendous boost to the GAA in America and be the launching-pad, as it were, for a revival in Gaelic games. At the Congress on 6 April the Canon proposed the Clare motion asking that the final be played in New York. That Congress was held on Easter Sunday and it coincided with the Railway Cup hurling final between Connacht and Munster, which had been deferred from St Patrick's Day because of the atrocious weather that spring — one of the semi-finals (Munster v Ulster) had been played only on the eve of Patrick's Day. During the afternoon the Congress was adjourned to allow the delegates to get to Croke Park for the hurling match and it appears that before the adjournment there were few signs of enthusiasm for Canon Hamilton's proposal. But whatever happened during the break for the hurling final there was very big support for the idea when the Congress re-assembled that evening in the Croke Park offices. When the motion was passed by much more than the necessary two-thirds majority a new chapter in GAA history was about to be written. Congress decided to ask the Central Council to investigate the feasibility of staging the game in New York. Although I had visions of a trip to the States I must say that I still doubted if the game would ever reach New York — even when the Executive Committee (now called the Management) agreed to send the general secretary Paddy O'Keeffe and the secretary of the Connacht Council Tom Kilcoyne to New York to investigate the possibility of a final in America.

You must realise that trans-Atlantic travel was just starting up again after the war and the steamships and the few propeller planes going to America were heavily booked out transporting the military and their families back to the US. Both O'Keeffe and Kilcoyne had to travel by the Holyhead mailboat and then by ship from Southampton to get to America for their investigation. When they returned the general secretary told a meeting of the Central Council on 23 May that one steamship company could offer no accommodation and another would take only 25 passengers going out but had 60 places for the return journey. This led to a lengthy discussion as to whether the players should be asked to travel by air, which was by no means the commonplace mode of travel it is today. Indeed the president of the association, Dan O'Rourke from Roscommon, stated 'that the responsibility of sending some of the party by air was too great for the Council' and, while he was prepared to travel by air he would not vote that anyone else should go by air. However, the council eventually voted 20 to 17 that the teams should travel by whatever means were available — mostly after a passionate plea by Mícheál Ó Ruairc of Kerry that they as a national organisation should be advocating that people use Rineanna airport (as Shannon was then called), which was then just being developed. The two officials, O'Keeffe and Kilcoyne, in their report stated that the famous Yankee Stadium would not be suitable, but the other baseball ground in the Bronx suburb of New York, the Polo Grounds, which was then the home of the New York Giants, could provide a playing area for Gaelic football of 137 yards long and 84 yards wide. By 23 votes to 12 the council agreed that the Polo Grounds should be the venue.

By now I had decided that this was such an important game that it would have to be broadcast and I was vain enough to assume that I would be the one for the job. However at that time Radio Éireann had never broadcast any event of any kind from America and being then directly under the aegis of the Department of Post and Telegraphs, and so an arm of the civil service, they had to go to the Department of Finance for the money to finance the venture. The Director of Broadcasting, Seamus Ó Braonáin, had won four All-Ireland football medals with Dublin in the early years of the century and he was enthusiastic about booking the radio lines for a broadcast to be done by one Michael O'Hehir. But the story is told that when he met the then secretary of the Department of Finance to ask for finance, which Radio Éireann themselves didn't have, he was asked: 'Seamus, tell me does anybody listen to these football matches?'

Eventually after much ado, it was decided that the radio station would take care of the cost of the broadcast lines while the GAA would pay the expenses of bringing me to America and cover the costs of my stay there. So I was soon told: 'Get your passport and visa, your dollars and be sure you get vaccinated.' Passport, visa and dollars were easy, but the vaccination — that's a different story. In those days it was essential and you carried a vaccination certificate signed by your doctor to confirm that you had been immunised against smallpox. 'There's nothing to it,' I told everybody, 'It's just a pin prick and it's over.' Oh, how wrong I was!

As the racing correspondent with the *Irish Independent* I was in Tramore two days later and in such obvious pain that a friend, Tom Fleming, called a doctor and I was landed in hospital for penicillin injections. I didn't sit down comfortably for a few days afterwards. Despite the discomfort I felt it would be worth it when I arrived in the New World because, like most of those travelling on this great adventure, it would be my first trip across the Atlantic.

Some of us had to be in Croke Park on Sunday, 7 September, for the hurling final in which Kilkenny beat Cork with Terry Leahy's last-minute point (0-14 to 2-7). We had hoped to fly to Shannon afterwards, but some crux arose and instead we set out by car. My travelling companions were Henry O'Mahony from Cork, chairman of the Munster Council, and Mitchel Cogley, Fred's father and the sports editor of the *Irish Independent*, who always maintained afterwards that my mother sprinkled us all with holy water when we were leaving the O'Hehir house just to make sure that everything would be all right.

The *Irish Press* by the way didn't send a sports journalist to cover the trip. Instead they assigned Anna Kelly, the editor of their woman's page, to fly out with the teams, but they had Arthur Quinlan from Limerick actually cover the All-Ireland final. Arthur, who was to become a journalistic institution in the south-west, was on an extended stay in New York at the time and, as he had already been a regular contributor to the *Irish Press* before leaving for America, he was commissioned to report the big match. There had, of course, been intense interest in the championship that summer because of the prize of a trip to New York for the two All-Ireland finalists. The whole thing had captured the imagination of the public and frequently cars were seen going to matches bedecked not only in the occupants' county colours but also displaying the Stars and Stripes. Huge crowds turned up at all the games and the two semi-finals attracted large numbers of spectators — 60,075 at the Cavan-Roscommon game on 4 August was over 8,000 up on the previous semi-final record (Roscommon v Laois in 1946) and a week later there were still more (65,939) at the Kerry-Meath clash. Despite having won so many honours the Kerrymen were more determined than ever to qualify for the appearance in New York where so many of their countymen had made their homes. Cavan got goals from Peter Donohoe and Tony Tighe to beat Roscommon.

On 3 September the first contingent set sail across the Atlantic aboard the *SS Mauretainia* from Cobh — seven players and two officials from each of the two competing counties. The rest of the party, 40 in total, flew out from Shannon and only a handful of us had ever been in an airplane previously, none of us across the Atlantic, so it was an exciting adventure for us all. But a mighty lengthy one. On arrival in Shannon we were told that our TWA Skymaster the 'Maulmein Pagoda,' would be 12 hours late taking-off. To get to America these days you hop on a plane in Shannon and arrive in New York seven hours later. How different it was in 1947. We had been told the winds from the south west would necessitate us taking on extra fuel in the Azores, the Portuguese possession about one-third of the way to the US. So we had a 45-minute stop in Santa Maria and had to surrender our passports to the Portuguese officials who spoke only very limited broken English. Their efforts to pronounce some of the Irish names when handing back the passports gave us many laughs with the highpoint being when one official called out for 'Meester Tigee' meaning Mr Tighe. Tony collected his passport but the great Cavan wing forward was stuck with the nickname 'Tigee' all through the trip.

Non-stop trans-Atlantic flights weren't possible in those days, so the next leg had us in Gander in Newfoundland nine hours later. As we came in to land we could see the huge forests, the winding rivers with their huge logs floating down to camps, the rough rocky hills and even the ice. As we walked across the tarmac we were hit by the chill in the air and soon we were hit by the news that one of the plane's engines was off-key! So we spent another two hours walking around a somewhat dismal airport. Back in the air we had one more stop to make: this was in Boston where US medical officers checked out our vaccination certificates and then we were allowed to leave the plane for a few minutes. And the heat was almost overwhelming — in stark contrast to the cold in Newfoundland. We were greeted by a reception committee from the Boston GAA and a group of newspapermen. But soon we were off again and at last the dream came true: NEW YORK! Our landing was at La Guardia airport as Idlewild (later to become

JFK) still hadn't come into service as the major overseas airport for New York.

Here we were in the city of skyscrapers — 29 hours after leaving Shannon. The group that had gone by boat arrived the previous day (8 September) and some of them were at the airport along with the president of the GAA, Dan O'Rourke, to greet us. When we reached downtown Manhattan the party split up — Kerry to the Henry Hudson hotel, Cavan to the Empire and myself and Mitchel Cogley with some officials to the Hotel Woodstock where Paddy O'Keeffe, who had left Ireland several weeks before, and John 'Kerry' O'Donnell and other officials had set up an office as the game headquarters and ticket centre. They worked from early morning to late at night. It was there I met John Kerry for the first time and I will never, ever forget the tremendous amount of work that man put into making a success of this great venture. The mayor of New York was Bill O'Dwyer, a native of Bohola in Co. Mayo and his office had organised a reception at City Hall the following day for the teams and officials following a traditional ticker-tape parade down Broadway in a large fleet of cars escorted by police motorbike outriders with screaming sirens. A scene out of many movies we had seen, but now we were experiencing it at firsthand. Crowds lined the streets behind barriers and probably no more than a handful knew who the 'guys' being honoured were. But with the ceremonies over it was down to the serious business for the teams; Kerry went training in John O'Donnell's Croke Park (later to be renamed Gaelic Park) and Cavan had a work out in the public Van Cortlandt Park.

There was something of a shock at the Kerry session when Paddy Kennedy, their great midfielder, didn't tog-out to train. He had been injured in the semi-final against Meath and as the week went on in New York he was regarded as very doubtful and the Kerry selectors were delaying naming their team until the very last minute. As the excitement built up around our hotels and among the Irish who came visiting us, I began to realise the immense responsibility resting upon me as the representative of the many thousands at home who would normally be at this All-Ireland final had it been in Dublin. Therefore I paid a visit to the Polo Grounds at 157th Street and St Nicholas Avenue in the Bronx to see that everything was in order. The famous stadium, which had housed many great events including world heavyweight fights, was still the home ground of the Giants baseball team — the club was to move to Candlestick Park in San Francisco in1958 and the Polo Grounds soon to be demolished and replaced by an apartment complex. What's more, in September the baseball season was still in progress, so you can imagine my amazement on the Friday when I discovered the pitcher's mound — a hump on the ground several inches high — was still on the pitch. I remember Martin O'Neill, the secretary of the Leinster Council and a former footballer and handballer who was out to referee the final, saying: 'They hadn't taken away the mound a few days before the match when Paddy O'Keeffe and I went to the Polo Grounds to look at the ground and the groundsman was showing us around. "Oh," I says, "this thing [the mound] has to be taken out of here, you couldn't play a match here." The lad nearly went berserk.' However, despite Martin's reservations the pitcher's mound remained in place on Sunday — and it was only one of the disadvantages the players had to contend with. The heat of over 85°F was another. I, on the other hand, suddenly discovered I had a big problem. The caretaker showed me the broadcasting booth from which the baseball broadcasts were done, but to my astonishment there were no wires to be seen anywhere to suggest that the required broadcast lines from the international telephone exchange had been installed. Panic! The caretaker knew nothing about a broadcast, so I hastened back to the hotel and immediately told Paddy O'Keeffe that no provision seemed to have been made for the broadcast. It even looked as if I might not have anything to do on the Sunday. Needless to say this was a story too good for Mitchel Cogley to pass up and he informed his readers in the Saturday *Evening Herald* and the *Sunday Independent* that there was a possibility of the final not being broadcast. This caused consternation at home, we later heard, not least in Radio Éireann who confirmed to the GAA general secretary O'Keeffe that the lines had been properly booked and the Columbia Broadcasting System (CBS) were responsible for the arrangements. CBS, however, declared they were obliged only to install the microphones and other sound equipment only on the day and that the telephone company (AT&T) were the ones charged with putting in the relay lines. Believe me, there were many urgent phone calls made that evening and on the Saturday morning and more than one cable message rushed across the Atlantic. Even on Saturday there remained some doubt about the broadcast because the London international telephone exchange was also involved — in those days all phonecalls from Ireland to the US were routed through London — and between RÉ, London and the AT&T there appeared to be a fall-down... and a Saturday was not the best day to try and get things rectified. However, the intercession of Mayor Bill O'Dwyer was sought by O'Keeffe and, happy outcome, at one o'clock New York time on the Saturday Paddy was assured that the lines would be installed on his payment of the required costs, which I understand were later re-imbursed by RÉ.

So what really happened? Blame was being placed all around; fingers were pointed at Radio Éireann, the London exchange and even the American Telephone and Telegraph Company. Therefore, it should be recorded that Paddy O'Keeffe told the Central Council at a meeting in December 1947 when presenting his comprehensive report on the final, that AT&T accepted that the fault was theirs. The general secretary said that he had received 'an unsolicited letter' from an executive at AT&T he had been dealing with in New York. It stated: 'While the results were satisfactory from a broadcasting standpoint I am afraid there might not have been a broadcast at all had it not been for your thoughtfulness in calling me when you did as time was running out ... Your call brought to light a message sent from London the week before wherein we were instructed to provide the service but which, I am sorry to say, was misinterpreted by our people and on which no action was taken.'

But back in September all that mattered to me was the relief when I was told that the broadcast could go ahead as the lines were being laid on. The final was due to start at half past three and the lines were reserved until 5 p.m. which we thought, in our innocence, would give us plenty of time.

On the morning of the match all the party were received at St Patrick's Cathedral by Cardinal Spellman and after Mass I went early to the Polo Grounds. The heat was stifling, there was dead, damp humidity and the concrete-like pitch was being watered by the automatic sprinkler system we had all admired when we saw it working a few days before. But the sod — a little grass and lots of clay — was still baked hard. The senior game was preceded by a curtain-raiser between two local teams of American-born minors and long before 3 o'clock the referee, Martin O'Neill, and the four provincial officers who were his umpires — Henry O'Mahony (Munster), Gerry Arthurs (Ulster), Tom Kilcoyne (Connacht) and Jack Brennan (Connacht) took the field. Soon afterwards the teams came on the field to a great roar from the crowd of 34,941 who paid $153,877 (then worth £38,469) and that, local officials told us, would have been much bigger but for heavy rain the previous evening. Kerry had delayed announcing their team until the last minute because of Paddy Kennedy's injury and he eventually lined-out (unusually) at left full-forward with Eddie Dowling partnering Gega O'Connor at midfield.

It developed into a sensational contest. How the teams lasted in the intense heat is beyond me. I had started without a tie in the broadcast box and by half-time my soaked shirt was almost off and halfway through the second half it was off. Yet the teams played like men inspired and thrilled us all in as hectic an hour as I have seen. Each one of our 'ambassadors' did the country proud and played every second of the game like true sportsmen. Did I say sensational? Kerry were quickly a goal and a point up with Gega O'Connor opening the scoring and Batt Garvey soon having a goal. Then in the tenth minute Eddie Dowling got through for another one and it was 2-1 to 0-1 and the prospect of a very one-sided game when Kerry went seven points up after 12 minutes. Halfway through the first half Cavan fell eight points behind, but then that great-hearted team started to fight back. Peter Donohoe kicked three points and Kerry didn't score again before the interval. Cavan did — and how! In the 28th minute Joe Stafford went through for a goal and then Mick Higgins, who had been born in New York and was now playing in his home town, added another. So what a change about it was when the half-time score read: Cavan 2-5, Kerry 2-4.

This was a marvellous game to broadcast. Within seconds of the restart Gega O'Connor equalised for Kerry, but Peter Donohoe kicked two points to put Cavan two in front by the seventh minute of the half. O'Connor pointed, Donohoe hit back with one for Cavan and the tension was palpable when Gega narrowed the gap to only one point, 2-8 to 2-7. The suspense was mounting by the second as Kerry strove to get back and they had about ten minutes left according to my watch. But, to my horror, the stadium clock told me that it was five minutes to five. With a jolt I realised that the match would not finish by 5 o'clock, the designated time at which the booking for the radio lines would run out. Now the fact that the match didn't start as planned was proving costly. Between bishops, commissioners for this and that, and presidents of the GAA and New York being introduced to the crowd things had run late. Mayor O'Dwyer had to be welcomed onto the field also before he threw in the ball. More time was lost at half-time when the mayor and the president of the GAA came to the broadcasting box to send greetings to the listeners at home and Kerry, obviously indulging in intense team discussions in the dressing-room, were a little slow coming back onto the field. And we had expected to have a little leeway at the end to describe the presentation of the cup before wrapping-up and handing back to the Radio Éireann studios in Dublin. The best laid plans...! Now I really started to sweat; I was convinced that the awful possibility of the broadcast ending before the match finished was about to happen. Obviously someone somewhere along the line had a piece of paper that said the lines to Ireland were to close at 5 p.m. and here we were with the two teams still locked in a hectic struggle. Can you imagine the uproar, the anger, in Ireland if we had gone off the air with a few minutes left to play?

Such was the excitement of the game that I had been talking at fever pitch throughout that second half. Now I became frantic and started pleading to whoever was in charge to give us five minutes more. I was begging, but not knowing if anyone in charge of the radio lines was listening in. I knew it would knock the bottom out of a great occasion if people in Ireland didn't hear the end of the match. If that happened I'm not sure I would have come home — well, maybe in disguise! Thankfully there was some American who realised the importance of the occasion to us; although I never discovered who that person was. He (or she) kept the lines open until six minutes past five. But as Peter Donohoe sent Cavan two points in front with nine minutes to go I had no way of knowing if we were still being heard in Ireland. Mick Higgins tacked on two more points and Kerry now needed a goal badly. And then it looked they might get it. Danger loomed for Cavan when sub Tim Brosnan bore down on the Cavan goalmouth and had only goalie Vincent Gannon to beat, but he crashed the ball off the crossbar. Cavan were champions again after a gap of 12 years. Cavan 2-11, Kerry 2-7.

You can imagine the riotous celebrations they had that night at the banquet in the Commodore Hotel which was attended by 1,400 people. By the time I got to that reception I still didn't know if Ireland had heard the end of the match, but a phone call home set my mind at rest — I was told the good news that we had got 'the five minutes more.' There was one very relieved commentator at that banquet.

Cables started arriving from Ireland during the dinner for the teams and the GAA officials and the broadcast was mentioned favourably in several of these. Later on that night I celebrated on Broadway with a very big American ice cream. The following day the New York papers were full of the big game. Peter Donohoe was the top scorer with eight points and Arthur Daley of the *New York Times*, the dean of that city's sportswriters, called Peter 'the Babe Ruth of Gaelic football.' In a city that adored the great Yankee's baseball star of the 1930s Peter could hardly have been paid a higher compliment. After the match Mitchel Cogley told me that my commentary had been relayed into the Press box at the Polo Grounds — supposedly as a help to the local sportswriters who were seeing Gaelic football for the first time. It must have gone well because two days later Dan Parker, another of the famous New York journalists of the time gave me a grand write-up in his New York *Daily Mirror* column.

On Tuesday morning I had an early start to get to the Twentieth Century Fox (New York) building where a selected party had been invited to view 40 minutes of a film that the GAA had commissioned, but which had to be reduced to just over ten minutes. I stayed on with two film folk who knew the business inside out but who had no idea what to leave in and what to take out. So, for over two days, while the rest of the party were enjoying the sights of New York, I was in the studios helping to cut, edit and put a voice-over narration on the film which I only saw in completed form back home in the Adelphi Cinema.

How was the radio commentary received here in Ireland? The day after the final the *Irish Independent* wrote that the most popular men around Dublin 'were those motorists with car radios, who remained parked in the streets and shared their enjoyment with appreciative audiences.' The article added: 'The biggest radio audience in the history of the GAA and Radio Éireann was chalked up last night.' A column in the *Irish Press* was particularly generous to the commentator, who they stated was one of the heroes of the hour to every excited listener here at home. 'Thanks to his descriptive powers we found ourselves beside him in the commentator's box gazing down upon a sun-baked pitch with a sea of 40,000 white-clad American fans on every side… Thanks Micheal we are all grateful for your wonderful broadcast.' Believe me, all of that more than compensated for the worry and anxiety of those 'five minutes more.'

All's well that ends well. We got the extra time and, as already stated, AT&T took the blame for the worry about the lines being booked on the eve of the final. On 22 September Mitchel Cogley and myself flew back to Ireland — a journey in sharp contrast to the flight out because it took only 12 hours to Shannon. A week later the rest of the party arrived in Southampton by boat and then travelled from Holyhead to Dun Laoire, arriving home on the night of 2 October. On the Sunday they were received by the president, Sean T. O'Kelly, and An Taoiseach, Eamon de Valera after a parade through Dublin and that night they were guests of the Central Council at a banquet in the Gresham Hotel. Needless to say I rejoined them to see out the expedition to the end. It was a great adventure and a trip that was one of the outstanding memories of my career. I enjoyed every moment of it. Yet, as always, I felt a sense of joy at being back in dear old Ireland again.

You see, there were family, friends and a certain lady named Molly Owens waiting.

* * *

About a year after the Second World War ended I was formally introduced to Molly Owens. We already knew each other to see as we had grown up and lived not far from one another in Drumcondra. My father and Molly's uncle, Seán Clancy, were fellow-Claremen and being keen GAA followers often met up at Croke Park. It was on one such occasion that I got talking to Miss Owens and was immediately smitten. She had just graduated from the College of Catering and Hotel Management in Cathal Brugha Street and was working as a receptionist in the Clarence Hotel on the quays. The romance blossomed and in 1948 we were married in Corpus Christi Church on Griffith Avenue. We were to fly to London that afternoon en route to Bournemouth where we were to spend our honeymoon but, as luck would have it, Dublin Airport was fog bound and there were no flights in or out that day. My good friend, Des Kerr, came to the rescue and offered to put us up for the night in his place at Summerseat near Clonee. His brother Fergus was the best man at our wedding and subsequently became the godfather to our eldest son, Tony. Des had to go to his office first, though, and to fill in the time we went to the show in the Theatre Royal. Hoping not to be noticed, we sneaked into the back row of the stalls but moments later I felt a tap on the shoulder. It was Eamonn Andrews, then the compere of the very popular 'Double or Nothing' segment of the show. He said: 'Come with me, we'll give you a nice box where you won't be disturbed.' Innocently, we followed him and sat there happily until the show was over. Then, of course, Eamonn appeared on stage and, directing the spotlight right on us, said… 'Look who we have here' or words to that effect. Of course, we had to stand up and take a bow. Oh, the embarrassment of it all! We eventually made it to Bournemouth, a little out of season, admittedly, and, not being one to miss an opportunity, I made sure we took in the Aintree November meeting on the way home.

As with most newly-weds money was in short supply when we first set up house in Grace Park Road but I was able to supplement my pay packet from Independent Newspapers — I think I was on about nine guineas a week — with my broadcasting work including the nightly Hospitals' Sweeps racing bulletin so we managed. Tony, our first-born, arrived in 1950, Mary a year later and when Mike came along it was becoming a bit crowded in Grace Park Road so we began to look around for a bigger house.

We considered moving out of town but as Molly was, in effect, like myself, an only child — her two brothers had emigrated to Australia by this time — we were reluctant to go too far away from our parents. It was my mother who found the house of our dreams. She had often admired it as she walked past on her way to Grace Park Road and one day she heard it was to be put up for sale. Number 206 Griffith Avenue was owned by Mrs Monahan, mother of the actress Peg Monahan. Her family had all gone away, she was moving to a smaller abode, and we bought it for £3,500. It was in a very pleasant location, backing onto the farm attached to All Hallows College which afforded a degree of privacy and a nice rural feel. Incidentally, the seminary farm was run in those days by a Mr Ahern, whose son Bertie was to make a name for himself in later life.

Before we moved to our new address Molly insisted that something had to be done with the kitchen which to her professionally trained eye was totally inadequate. There was no problem. We sent for two friends of mine, Norman Allen and 'Snitchie' Ferguson, outstanding members of St Vincent's and Dublin teams of that time, who had gone into business together as building contractors. They did a fine job, refurbishing the bathroom and kitchen, all for £500.

We were nicely set up now. But for me life just got more and more hectic and there was a price to pay. While I criss-crossed the country week after week, year after year from one race meeting to another and then on Sundays to Semple Stadium or Tuam, to Casement Park or the Cork Athletic Grounds the children were growing up fast and far too often I could not be around when I would liked to have been.

4

They Were The Boys of Wexford

Old friends, it's said, are best. But in the life of a sports commentator I'm not sure that's always true; indeed, I've often felt it was otherwise. While one admires great champions and great stars, and is thrilled to see them proving themselves again and again, there is a huge element of excitement infused into a sport when 'new faces' come along. The emergence of new champions and new teams gives great pleasure — except, that is, to the supporters of the deposed sides the newcomers overcome to reach the top. A change in the established order is welcomed and I've always been delighted when a new team comes to the forefront in hurling or football. Perhaps the side that all of us connected with Gaelic games gave the warmest welcome to was the marvellous Wexford hurling team of the 1950s.

It is hardly correct to describe Wexford as 'new' to hurling prominence although their 1950s team was a revelation and brought about a major change in the fortunes and affiliations of Wexford. More correctly, this wonderful team changed Wexford from being a football county to a hurling county — at least as far as success on the field was concerned.

From the earliest years of the GAA Wexford had always been one of the stronger dual counties producing teams of equal proficiency at hurling and football. The hurling team won the All-Ireland championship in 1910 and their last Leinster championship in 1918, the year the county completed the first ever four-in-a-row in the All-Ireland football championship — a feat that would stand as a record for 14 years until Kerry won four in succession from 1929 to 1932.

Thereafter Wexford's hurling fortunes declined and they reached the Leinster final only twice — beaten by Dublin in 1944 and Kilkenny in

1950. Meanwhile the football teams enjoyed not much better success — two provincial championships in 1925 and 1945 — by comparison, but by the 1950s Wexford had been established in the public's perception as a football county. Then along came Nicky Rackard.

The Rackard home was on the site of the house once lived in by John Kelly, the Boy from Killane and the patriot of the 1798 Insurrection. An uncle of theirs, John Doran, had played football with Wexford in 1918 when the county won that fourth consecutive championship.

As the Rackards grew up there was no hurling club in Rathnure, the area they were later to make famous around the hurling world. But the game played a very large part in their childhood because the tradition of hurling was still strong in most of the rural areas in Wexford. The Rackards' father, Robert, was keenly interested in horses and was a prominent huntsman in his day who bred and kept many horses. As Nicky once declared: 'The two ruling passions of our young lives were horses and hurling. There was only one way to get us away from hurling and that was to send us to look after the horses.'

From an early age Nicky showed a tremendous proficiency at hurling and had just turned 13 in 1935 when he made his debut on the Rathnure minor team, the first minor side ever fielded by the club. The following year he was enrolled in St Kieran's College, Kilkenny, as a boarder — the choice of the Kilkenny institution rather than a college in Wexford was explained by the fact that the sons of a great family friend who visited Killane frequently were also entering St Kieran's that year. To someone as mad about hurling as he was St Kieran's amounted to an arrival in Paradise itself.

In his second year he was picked on the college junior team and in January 1938 anyone at a Leinster junior semi-final in Nowlan Park got a preview of what was to become a common occurrence — Nicky Rackard scoring a profusion of goals. Playing against Ballyfin College that day he accounted for five goals and was soon promoted to the St Kieran's senior team for a replay against Coláiste Caoimhin from Dublin. During his stay in the Kilkenny college neither their senior nor junior team suffered a defeat. This may not have been considered exceptional in the case of any of the students from Co. Kilkenny who would have been so accustomed to their county winning matches at all levels. But to someone from Wexford, which hadn't enjoyed hurling success for so long and had languished in Kilkenny's shadows for generations, this was of enormous significance. It set Nicky Rackard's mind aflame and he returned to Wexford with a burning desire to see his county succeed and with a proselytizing zeal to spread the hurling gospel around the county. Rackard had been a winner at St Kieran's and he could see no reason why Wexford hurlers couldn't be winners also.

There had been some splendid football teams in the county and people like Billy Rackard and Padge and Paddy Kehoe had also played on the football team. They were among a group of young hurlers coming through the ranks, inspired by the elder Rackard brother, and there were some marvellous county finals around the end of the 1940s between St Aidan's (Enniscorthy) and Rathnure St Anne's and they also had Cloughbawn with players such as Tim Flood. Soon they were an emergent force on the county scene and by 1950 they were able to run Kilkenny to a goal.

There was a large family of Rackards and four of the brothers played for the emergent Wexford team in 1951 — Jimmy in goal, Billy and Bobby in defence and Nicky as the full-forward. It is safe to say — with no reflection on the great hurling ability of the others, especially Billy and Bobby — that Nicky was the supreme Rackard, not only the inspirational leader for the rest, but the most influential personality of modern times on Wexford hurling itself. I came to know him well over the years as a hurling figure, both player and selector, and as a person deeply involved in racing, both as a breeder and owner. He was an extraordinary man: huge in stature, strong and with a single-minded determination, but a big-hearted lovable personality who was an admirable sportsman on the field. Indeed, one of the outstanding traits of the great Wexford teams of the 1950s was their great sportsmanship and gallantry on the field even though they were physically a big team. They took great pride in their reputation as a sporting side. The sad feature of Nicky Rackard's life was that he was never more deeply admired than in his later years when he publicly admitted his problems with drink and went public about his battle against alcoholism. He then devoted most of his attention and energies — just as earnestly as he had to hurling in earlier times — to helping other sufferers of alcoholism to overcome their problems as he had done with the help of the AA organisation.

In 1951 Wexford won their first provincial hurling championship in 33 years and went on to reach the All-Ireland final despite being taken to a first round replay by Meath. But it was probably too much to expect them to succeed the first time up for an All-Ireland final. Especially since they were playing against the Tipperary team that had already won the championship for the previous two years. Then they had to wait another three years to get back to the final. They were gaining in experience all the time and some like Art Foley (in goal) and Seamus Hearne (midfield) had come into the team in the meantime and Ned Wheeler had moved from midfield to left half-back. They were now a stronger unit, much more mature in the ways of top-class competition but, yet again, they met one of the more predominantly successful teams when Cork were their opponents in the All-Ireland final.

It was a Cork team peppered with some of the most celebrated names in hurling: Ring, of course, Tony O'Shaughnessy a stocky, but great corner back, two magnificent half-backs, Matt Fouhy and Vince Twomey, and a forward division that included Christy as the captain, Willie John Daly, Josie Hartnett and the relative youngsters, Eamonn Goulding and Johnny Clifford. It was Wexford's ill-luck that, once again as with Tipperary in 1951, they faced a team going for three-in-a-row in the championship, Cork having already won the title in 1952 and 1953. The Leinster champions were also unlucky in that they lost their big full-back, the Kilkenny native Nick O'Donnell, who although from the Noreside county contributed so much to Wexford's resurgence. Early in the second half Nick had to retire with an injured shoulder.

The winning goal was scored by Johnny Clifford, who has continued to play a leading role in Cork hurling even down to recent times as a manager and selector. I remember talking to both Billy Rackard and Johnny about it. Billy recalled: 'I felt I was the weak man on the Wexford team that day: I was playing in a position I hated, corner back, and Paddy Barry was a strong man on the Cork team, but it transpired that I was holding him to my surprise. Somebody spotted it, Jim Barry maybe, and Paddy moved off me. He switched corners and then the goal came. I made a mistake. I had a frightful guilty conscience about it for a long time.'

Johnny Clifford had just turned 20 before this, his first All-Ireland final, and he remembered: 'Paddy and I weren't getting anything out of Billy Rackard and Mick O'Hanlon, the man I was on. So Joe Hartnett eventually asked us to switch. At that time the selectors were Sean Óg Murphy [the county secretary], Fox Collins and Dinny Barry Murphy and, Lord have mercy on us, you daren't do a thing like that — switch yourselves — with those people. But we did and lucky enough I got the break. I remember Billy left me alone for a few minutes and went out to challenge with Ring and Jim English; Ring beat them both and I just happened to be on the spot.'

Wexford did eventually win the title in 1955, but for me 1956 was the greatest year for Wexford hurling and this team. Not only did they win the All-Ireland final — and had their revenge on Cork — but they captured the National League. Not only did they win the National League but did so in the most dramatic fashion with a remarkable second-half comeback in one of the most astonishing matches I've ever seen. It will always be remembered as 'The Day of the Big Wind'. Tipperary in those times were regarded as the National League specialists and by half-time of the final, played on 7 May 1956, they had established a lead of 15 points — 2-10 to 0-1. Wexford looked to be in for the worst hiding in the history of the League final. But the commentator sees only what is happening on the field; up in my radio commentary box I didn't know what was happening in the Wexford dressing-room.

Down the years there have been many stories, perhaps many exaggerated, about captains or trainers giving memorable and very effective talks at half-time in dressing-rooms. But there is no doubt that the one Nicky Rackard gave — or, to be more accurate, inflicted upon — his Wexford team-mates during the interval of that League final is now legendary in the folklore of hurling. And it did happen: he launched into a harangue with venom and vehemence, we learned afterwards, and didn't pull any punches in his comments on his colleagues. I remember his brother Billy many years later saying: 'It's very easy to say that a pep talk worked after a win like we eventually had in that match. But it was a very good pep talk and Nicky was very good at that sort of thing. He could get very emotional and he could, how do you say, be very aggressive or produce whatever ingredients are necessary for a pep talk. He was pretty good at it. He banged the stick off the dressing-room floor, but I'm sure it's been done a hundred times since without the same effect. I don't want to knock pep talks: they are essential, but that's one to be remembered, I will say.'

Nothing had worked in the first half for Wexford. Billy also remembered: 'Apart altogether from the wind, we couldn't get into the game. We couldn't get to the Tipperary fellows. Leave out the wind, we were still behind as everything was going wrong.'

Remember, for the second half Wexford now had the gale behind them and within minutes the miraculous recovery was under way. Soon after the throw-in Nicky went through for a goal and then his handpass deceived Tipp's goalkeeper Tony Reddan and Tom Ryan finished the ball to the net. There was enormous pressure building up on Tipperary and positional switches Wexford had made along with the introduction of Paddy Kehoe were beginning to work. Still we wondered if Wexford had the time to come back. Tom Dixon got their third goal after Nicky and Padge Kehoe combined to set him up, but even then Tipp were four points in front (2-14 to 3-7) with only nine minutes to go. Dramatic it had been up to that, but from there to the end it was extraordinary and I'm convinced that many of the 49,000 at that final still probably can't quite believe what they saw that day. Can you imagine what it was like for the commentator trying to keep up with the sensational happenings and bring the mounting excitement to the radio listeners?

Padge reduced the lead with a point, Nicky got another point and then he lobbed in a 21-yard free which Dixon crashed to the net and, marvellous to behold, Wexford were a point ahead four minutes from the end. The puck-out was quickly returned by the now exuberant Wexford side and Nicky rampaged through for their fifth goal — and his second. So they turned a 15-point half-time deficit into a four-point victory — and, truly, we had never, ever seen a more astonishing match.

An interesting 'sidelight' on that match was the fact that the *Irish Press* was due to start publishing the 'Nicky Rackard Story' the week after the League final, It was written by their Gaelic games correspondent, the late Pádraig Puirséal, who had been a friend of Nicky's since their student days. Pádraig, or Paddy as we best knew him, freely confessed to feeling more than a little embarrassed at half-time when Wexford were so far behind and soon afterwards he would be printing such complimentary features about the principal character on that Wexford team. He wasn't looking forward to the next few weeks, he told us, but it all turned out happily in the end and — the serialisation of Rackard's story couldn't have come at a better time than immediately after that glorious victory.

Now that Wexford were the National League winners as well as the All-Ireland champions from the previous September, everybody was looking forward to the 1956 All-Ireland final once Wexford and Cork qualified. Could Wexford gain revenge for 1954? Or would the great Christy Ring add an amazing ninth All-Ireland medal? But we had to wait longer than usual for the answers. Cork had qualified for both the hurling and football finals, and for the camogie final, too, but that summer there had been a serious epidemic of polio in the region. After consultations with the Health Authorities the Central Council decided in mid-August to postpone the All-Ireland finals because of the huge numbers of supporters that would travel from Cork. The hurling final was subsequently re-fixed for 23 September, and the football final for 7 October.

Believe me, it was well worth the wait. It turned out to be one of the most absorbing matches for decades. The postponement, it seemed, appeared to create even greater anticipation in the public and a huge crowd attended — 83,096. This was the second highest for a hurling final — there had been 84,856 at the final two years previously between the same counties. Apart from those two Wexford-Cork finals there's never been another 80,000 crowd at the hurling final. And the spectators got full value for their money with a marvellous, majestic contest that produced many more scores than their meeting in 1954. Then it was 1-9 to 1-6 for Cork; now the score board read Wexford 2-14, Cork 2-8.

But before we got to that result we had many, many moments that were cherished for a long time afterwards. Wexford, now the champions from the previous year's triumph over Galway in the final, moved confidently into the lead from Tim Flood's opening point in the first minute and Padge Kehoe added a goal before Christy Ring got Cork's first point from a free. Wexford led at half-time (1-6 to 0-5), but about 19 minutes into the second half Cork drew level after goals by Ring and Paddy Barry (1-10 to 2-7) and then Christy put them ahead with a point. However, with ten minutes still to go that was the last score Cork were to get mainly because of some of the most spectacular goalkeeping Croke Park had ever seen. It will always be remembered as a huge personal triumph for Art Foley, Wexford's keeper, most especially for denying Christy a goal in the last few minutes.

Only three minutes remained and Cork were only two points behind when Paddy Philpott, Cork's left half-back, sent a long clearance upfield. It reached Ringey, who had moved away from Bobby Rackard, and when he careered away towards goal Wexford's lead looked to be severely threatened. He was about 20 yards out when he lashed a piledriver at Art Foley. Sensationally it was stopped! Wexford utterly relieved, Cork stunned to disbelief that the maestro hadn't smashed the ball to the net as he had done so often in a glorious career. Christy always believed in following up any shot and he went charging in. Was he about to send Art crashing to the net? To the great delight of Wexford fans and Christy's admirers everywhere, he was seen to 'compliment' Foley.

It was the match-winning save even though Cork came with another chance and Foley stopped it again. From the clearance the ball went to Nicky Rackard who got Wexford's second goal. The match was won and Ringey failed to get the ninth medal.

Art Foley's save has gone into the folklore of hurling and there have been many versions of what Ringey said to him when he chased in after his unsuccessful shot. Most of these became tall tales and grew in exaggeration as time went by. So nearly three decades later when RTE Radio did a series of programmes on my broadcasting career producer Ian Corr sought the views of Foley, who had long since gone to live in America.

The goalkeeper remembered: 'Everybody in the country told me how I saved it, but nobody asked me how DID I save it. Well, actually I blocked it with the hurl. The ball went straight up in the air. Then it was just like a camera: you're looking around to see who's around. [Josie] Hartnett and [Gerry] Murphy were coming in full belt, so I blocked it out to [Jim] Morrissey. Christy was full sure he had a goal and that's the whole idea of it. He came rushing in after it and when he saw the ball wasn't in the net the first thing he did was stuck out his hand and says 'you little black bastard, you're after beating us.' I'd say myself if I had let it go, or if I had missed it, I would have let the ball go over the bar because the ball was rising, going up high.'

In the amazing scenes after the final whistle three Wexfordmen — Foley, Bobby Rackard and Nick O'Donnell — chaired Christy Ring shoulder high off the field in a tremendous gesture of sportsmanship that was typical of that great Wexford team. They were a massive team, physically, and when one met them even many years afterwards we couldn't but be still amazed at the size of them. Yet, they were admired far and wide for the sportsmanship they showed on the field, never using their strength unfairly and very conscious of proper conduct at all times during games. The utterly sad thing is that the county never had a team like them again. Even though they took titles in the 1960s, they had, regrettably, been out of the roll of honour since 1968, which was far, far too long for a county like theirs.

Thankfully, the championship of 1996 has changed all that and there was much rejoicing when they won the Leinster championship again after 19 years of so much frustration in what was a splendid provincial final against Offaly — one of the best games of hurling we saw in what was a glorious summer for sport.

For so many years our hearts went out especially to the long-serving Wexford players like George O'Connor, Billy Byrne, Tom Dempsey and Martin Storey as they suffered disappointment after disappointment. Then along came Liam Griffin who has something of the same passion for hurling, Wexford hurling in particular, that the great Nicky Rackard had — and seemed to be consumed with a fervent desire to get, and keep, Wexford at the top of the hurling world. Not many of us had heard of Liam before his appointment as the county's manager, but there can't be anyone in the country who is now unaware of his existence after what he achieved in 1996 with his team. As the All-Ireland champions after an interval of 28 years the effect that triumph will have on the welfare of hurling in the county is probably incalculable. Let's hope sincerely that the benefits will be long lasting and the county never again drifts back into the trough of frustration they have suffered through for so long.

Of course, I kept meeting Nicky Rackard fairly frequently for many years afterwards through his interest in racing and when his playing career was finished he became more and more involved in racing. He was known to ride now and again and he bred and trained several horses. Tombrack, Ballyellis and Shining Flame were bred from his mare, Kibranish, and trained in Bunclody.

With his untimely death in 1976, at the age of 54, after a heroic battle against illness we lost not only a friend, but also a sportsman who was admired wherever hurling was known and appreciated. He was a hero who while still alive had gained legendary status in his native Wexford to rank with the many great historical figures that county has produced.

5

The Flying Doctor, Terrible Twins and True Blue Dubs

It goes without saying that commentators must strive at all times to be strictly neutral — no matter how deep-felt his affiliations to a particular county or how strong his friendships with members of a team. This is essential if you are to convey what is happening to listeners, or viewers, without imposing your own prejudices, as distinct from critical comments, during the broadcast. However, the commentator will find himself frequently being charged with bias by supporters of one team or another, more often than not by the fans of the team beaten in a big match. Believe me, this has happened to me during my career.

One evening shortly before Dublin played Galway in the 1963 All Ireland Football Final, the doorbell rang and I was told by one of the children that I was wanted at the hall door. A Dublin fan, on his way home from work, had called to complain that as a Dublin man I should be ashamed to be driving the maroon (Galway colours) coloured car he had seen parked in the driveway.

On another occasion, at an Ulster Final between Down and Cavan, a Down fan told me, in no uncertain fashion, that it was disgraceful I was driving a Cavan registered car! For the record I bought my cars from the late Maurice Jackson, a keen racing man, who was the main Ford dealer in Cavan. You can't win.

While most of the country was convinced I was a Dublin fan, first and foremost, events were to show that a certain, and let me quickly add, small section of Dublin supporters thought otherwise. One of my more frightening moments commentating came at Navan late on in my career after Meath had beaten Dublin in a game played at Pairc Tailteann when a group of so-called Dublin fans decided to give vent to their disappointment at the result by flinging stones and other missiles into the commentary box after the match. It was a very nasty experience.

Phrases such as 'Socks down around his ankles', 'He bends, he lifts, he strikes,' 'There's a schamozzle in the square' 'This game is young yet' were part and parcel of many of my match broadcasts. But other things said in the heat of the moment during a match were often misinterpreted by the listening public. If a game was one-sided I often used to say 'What this game needs is a goal for Cork (or Galway or Dublin or whatever team was losing.)' If that goal came and the complexion of the particular game changed then supporters of the opposing team often accused me of 'wishing defeat on them'.

My telephone number was always listed in the phone directory as I was in the communications business after all. But there were times when I wished otherwise. Late night calls, usually from pubs, to settle bets were a regular occurrence. Some questions were easily answered, but I was really dumbfounded one night when the phone rang and I was asked to settle a £50 bet by naming which team came out first for the second half of a National League Final which had been played over 20 years previously! Needless to say I had to pass on that one.

Another night, close to midnight, I received an extremely irate call from someone claiming to be a brother of a goalkeeper, who had let in a couple of 'soft' goals in a Munster Hurling Championship game, which I had commentated on earlier that day. During the commentary I had seemingly said something along the lines that the player in question had had better games and wouldn't have happy memories of the match in question. The caller was completely convinced that I had a 'set' against his brother and that it was my fault, and not the goalie's that the goals had gone in. He even went as far as claiming that my shouting in the commentary box during the more exciting stages of the game had distracted the goalkeeper!

The best indication of my impartiality was when the followers of both teams in a particular game accused me of being biased in favour of the other team. In a case like that you really couldn't win!

Having said all that I must admit to a certain affinity with the Mayo team that came into pre-eminence in the early 1950s by winning successive All-Ireland championships. Although I do hope it never showed in any of my commentaries I felt a little closer to this team than to most others because of a family connection with the county through my wife Molly and her brothers, Dick and Paddy Owens.

The Owenses were Dublin-born and lived in Clare Road, Drumcondra, quite close to the Hehirs in Ormond Road. Their Mayo connection came through an uncle of theirs, a Garda superintendent, who had served in Monaghan before moving to Castlebar. This was Dick Creagh, known as The Long-Kicker, who played football with Mayo in the late 1920s and early 1930s and was unfortunate enough to be just ahead of Mayo's magnificent string of six National Football League triumphs, which still stands as a record. The Owenses built a house in Lecanvey in Mayo and Molly and her brothers went down there every summer, a practice that has continued with her and the O'Hehirs to present times. Consequently, although Dublin-born she became a died-in-the-wool Mayo supporter and when our children came along the months of July and August were usually spent down in Lecanvey. Depending on my broadcasting commitments I spent as much time there with the family as possible and the month of July, with the Galway races and the Connacht football final, allowed me to slip over there regularly.

Incidentally, my family have reminded me how I used send them a coded message at the end of my broadcasts during the summer months when they were in Lecanvey in Mayo. I joined them there whenever possible, depending on where I was on the Sunday for a match and on what commitments I had the following week. So at the end of each commentary I would use a different sign-off phrase which would tell Molly whether I was or was not arriving in Mayo that night. Nothing like using the public airwaves for private messages! When the crowds were reported as heading out towards the Western Road this meant that I'd be on route to join the family. I also remember making use of the national television network via the weekly *Sport in Action* programme back in the 1960s and 1970s to pass on a message to my youngest son, Peter.

At that time he had already developed a keen interest in racing and was a fan of the late Michael Hurley who trained at the Curragh. Peter was interested in the exploits of one of Mick's horses – St Glin Glin at an evening meeting in Thurles one Thursday. I had promised that if the horse had won I would rub my nose immediately the programme restarted after the commercial break – I kept my word, rubbed my nose and Peter went off to bed a happy little boy.

As a result of my time in Lecanvey I got to know Mayo football people very, very well and would often drive in to see their teams training in Ballina or Castlebar. Despite those record-making six National Leagues and their 1936 All-Ireland success they were finding it harder and harder to get back into the big-time. But towards the end of the 1940s a new group of footballers, a new type of determined and ambitious player, came along and they were not prepared to let the county continue to languish in the football world.

The prime motivator was, of course, Sean Flanagan, who sadly died at the age of 71 in February 1993. Sean had gone to school in that great football nursery, St Jarlath's College, Tuam, and played minor with Mayo in 1940. But he missed that year's All-Ireland final when Mayo qualified to play Louth because he was 'incarcerated' as a clerical student just a few hundred yards up the road from Croke Park at Clonliffe College. In those days, clerics in all ecclesiastical institutions were not allowed breaks, even for a day, from the strict rigours of seminary life for anything as trivial as playing in an All-Ireland final — minor or senior. However, Sean's clerical life did not last too long and soon he entered UCD to study law. After playing for a time with the now-defunct Sean McDermott's club in Dublin he switched to the college team in the mid-1950s and captained the university to Sigerson Cup success.

He had by then been established on the Mayo senior team, but by 1947 had become very disillusioned with what was happening to Mayo football. In the 1947 Connacht championship the team was heavily beaten in the first round by Roscommon by nine points in May and long afterwards I heard him say: 'I was so disgusted by a collection of non-triers especially after what appeared to be apparent improvement over the previous two seasons. So I resigned from the team and it took a lot of persuasion to get me back again.'

It has long since been accepted that, to everyone's surprise, the turning point came on a very dreary November day in Tralee. That day (the 9th of the month) had started inauspiciously. Mayo football had hit such a low that none of the many selectors in the county had bothered travelling to Kerry for that National League match against the Munster champions. Only two weeks previously Kerry had got some revenge for their Polo Grounds defeat in New York by hammering Cavan in a special tournament at Croke Park that was watched by 35,000 people (4-8 to 1-6). Needless to say, not many people gave Mayo any hope and they were so short-handed in playing strength that Finn Mongey, the county secretary, and one of the drivers of a team car were asked to tog-out. The secretary and four players actually picked the team and most unexpectedly Mayo were only prevented from getting a very deserved win when Teddy O'Connor scored a late equalising point for the home team.

This was an eye-opening performance by the team, which unbelievably was not seen by even one selector, and this prompted five players who were based in Dublin to write a long no-punches-pulled letter to the county board. Padraic Carney, Sean Flanagan, Liam Hastings, Tom Langan and Eamonn Mongey stated that they felt the time had come 'when something must be done before football disappears completely in Mayo — unwept, unhonoured and unsung.' They demanded that the selection committee be reduced to five members who would attend all games and that the board arrange suitable challenge games against the counties in preparation for the championship. It is hard to credit nowadays that the county had anything from 16 to 20 selectors at that time.

Things began to happen and better organisation was introduced. It was also very important that Paddy Prendergast, who was living and playing in and with Donegal, declared for his native county and soon established himself as one of the game's greatest full-backs. Billy Kenny came back from Limerick and a young, towering Pat McAndrew was introduced into the team. Peter Quinn, a clerical student at Dalgan Park outside Navan, Peter Solan, Mick Flanagan and Sean Mulderrig also came into the team over the coming months. So, as Sean Flanagan once stated, they 'developed a genuinely good side in 1948 with six or seven who arrived in the previous 12 months.' He added: 'With the side we had in 1946 or 1947 we would not have ultimately got anywhere.' Where they did get was the All-Ireland final of 1948 — Mayo's first appearance in the final since they won the 1936 championship. It was a marvellous game, an eight-goal thriller in which Mayo were beaten by the defending All-Ireland champions Cavan by only one solitary point (4-5 to 4-4).

Mayo were desperately disappointed — maybe a little unreasonably so because they had not anything like the championship experience of their opponents. But it was a valuable lesson which matured them quickly and they soon proved their worth. Beaten by only one point in the final: that surely was a sign that Mayo would be back and, after a setback in 1949 when beaten in the All-Ireland semi-final by Meath, they were.

The 1950 campaign began in Carrick-on-Shannon with a win over Leitrim, then the Connacht final at Tuam against Roscommon and a very easy 12-point win over Armagh in the All-Ireland semi-final. Louth were the opponents in a final remembered as one of Sean Flanagan's best performances. Eamonn Mongey was also excellent at midfield beside Padraic Carney. After only five minutes Mayo suffered a terrible blow when centre half-forward Billy Kenny was carried off on a stretcher with a broken leg in an accidental clash and, sadly, the injury ended his football career. Eamonn Mongey recalls being near Billy when the accident happened and said 'As he left the pitch he rose from the stretcher and gave us a clenched fist signal which we all interpreted as 'no surrender' and I suppose it was for him as much as for ourselves that we won that match afterwards.'

Mayo, of course, by then were very well organised and, as was the practice then especially with teams that had several players living away from the county, the team was brought together in Ballina for a couple of weeks' collective training under former great players Gerald Courell and Jackie Carney.

It was a confident bunch of players who set out on the defence of the title in June 1951. Sligo were easily beaten, Galway hammered in Tuam and then the first meeting in the championship with Kerry since the 1948 semi-final. They played a draw and had to go back to Croke Park on 9 September for the replay — remember those were the days when the final was played on the fourth Sunday of September — and Kerry suffered one of its very few replay defeats.

Another Leinster team, Meath, awaited Mayo in the final and the Connacht champions wanted revenge for the 1949 defeat and the defeat only five months before in the League final. There were many heroes but none better than Mongey and John McAndrew at midfield, Peter Quinn on the half-back line, Carney now on the '40', who switched for a time with Mongey. and their great full-forward Tom

Langan, who scored a very important goal in the tenth minute, which was an equaliser and a tremendous early boost to Mayo. A legend, in fact, has gone into the folklore of football about that goal and what enabled Langan to score it. Before the Mayo team retired to bed in Barry's Hotel the night before the match Liam Hastings told Tom that Paddy O'Brien, the superb Meath full-back, could be beaten on his left side by a sidestep and that supposedly the Meathman was vulnerable to the sidestep. Langan went up to his bedroom with Hastings and they actually 'rehearsed' — that's Eamonn Mongey's word — the goal Tom got the next day! It seems Langan rolled up a towel into a ball and got Liam to act as the Meath full-back while Tom charged at him across the bedroom sidestepping and 'selling dummies' during this strange practice session.

Early in the final the next day Meath got off to a good start with three points and then ten minutes into the first half Langan got the ball out from the goalmouth and when he turned Paddy O'Brien was facing him. Langan swerved left and then right and was past the full-back. He hit a shot from about 20 yards that seemed to be going for the goalkeeper, Kevin Smyth, but curved away into the net at the last moment.

Mayo eventually won 2-8 to 0-9 with Carney the inspiration and their top scorer with five points and the second goal by Joko Gilvarry. The left half-back that day was Peter Quinn, who had been the No. 5 a year before. But if you were reading the newspapers on the morning after the 1951 final, or indeed were listening to my commentary, you wouldn't have known about Peter's second medal. Unless, that is, you were in the know! The wing back at that stage was now *Father* Peter Quinn, ordained earlier that summer as a member of the Columban Fathers (then known as the Maynooth Missions to China), and he was back at Dalgan Park studying languages before going to work in the Far East. Dalgan, as already stated, invoked the Maynooth Statutes which forbade clerics playing 'violent games' and Gaelic football was categorised as one of them. So there should have been no way P. Quinn, having played in 1950 as a clerical student, would be in the team the next year.

But as Peter in later years recalled, he was lucky to get out to play in the final. 'I told the county board officials how to get the permission for me,' he remembered. 'Not necessarily to talk to the local bishop in

Ballina or to the rector of the seminary but to get to the bishop of the diocese where the college was, which was Meath. Our two finals were against counties that came into his diocese so he couldn't very well say 'no I won't allow you to play' against Louth and Meath. But I had to change my name in case some busybody might ring the bishop and complain.' The result was that for the occasion Peter became 'P. Quinlan' and if you examine the daily papers for the next day you will see that the Mayo left half-back is recorded as P. Quinlan.

That was Mayo's last appearance in an All-Ireland final until 1989 when they lost to Cork and they have never again had a team as exceptional as the 1948–1951 side, which had so many talented footballers. They lost their Connacht crown in 1952 when beaten by Roscommon by eight points in the final and again were beaten in the provincial final by Roscommon in 1953. Galway knocked them out in the 1954 semi-final and by the time the provincial title was regained in 1955 some notables had departed the scene, goalkeeper Sean Wynne, John Forde, Peter Quinn, Henry Dixon, Padraic Carney and Joko Gilvarry.

During the 1930s Mayo had become known as 'The League Specialists' because of their sequence of six triumphs (1934–1939). They won the title again in 1941 and 1949 and the 1950s' team captured it again in 1954. That latter success has gone down in the lore of football because Padraic Carney earned the title 'The Flying Doctor' because of his part in the closing stages of that competition. The Swinford player had departed for an internship in New York early in the year after they had qualified for the semi-finals by beating Cavan in Castlebar. Dublin were the semi-final opponents and this new brand of young Dubs in the early 1950s were an impressive outfit. They had won the League in 1953 with 14 St Vincent's players plus Air Corps goalkeeper Tony O'Grady.

Facing this opposition the Mayo players recognised the need for their strongest team and that meant having Carney in the line-up. Now, flying the Atlantic in those days was nothing like the speedy jet travel we experience nowadays and in a propeller plane it could take anything up to 15 hours, which was quite an ordeal for Carney who flew in the day before the Dublin match. The players had persuaded the county board that his presence was essential and it surely was because when Mayo won 0-11 to 0-7 Padraic contributed seven points and struck up a great combination with his left flanker on the half-forward line, Eamonn Mongey, who returned to the team after missing the earlier matches in that league. Carlow qualified for the final by surprising Armagh and some people in Mayo felt that they would not need Padraic against such opposition, but he flew back from the US for the final also.

Sadly, it is now over 45 years since Mayo won the championship, but I must say the O'Hehir family wasn't the only one that had high hopes of that long void being bridged when John Maughan brought the county to the 1996 final. Unfortunately, there was grave disappointment when they failed despite playing so well against Meath in the draw and replay.

* * *

Just two months later the colours of the new National League champions of 1954 were lowered in a most unexpected fashion. Mayo were strong favourites going into the Connacht semi-final against Galway even though it was in Tuam Stadium. However, Galway had been rebuilding and new structures in the administration and organisation of Galway football were beginning to bear fruit. The county had a separate board for football and in 1952 Father Paddy Mahon, a priest from Dunmore at St Jarlath's College, became chairman of that Football Board. The exuberant enthusiasm of this young cleric with a passion for football allied to the vast experience and knowledge of people such as John 'Tull' Dunne and Brendan Nestor, two celebrated footballers of the past, brought changes. One of the most important of these was the start of a senior football league, which provided the clubs with much more real competition and enabled the players to maintain fitness at a reasonably high level all year round.

Galway had in those days still a great measure of experience in their team — Jack Mangan in goal, Tom Dillon and Sean Purcell. Purcell had been rated as one of the greatest of all colleges' players and even as a schoolboy had played in the 1946 colleges' final against St Patrick's, Armagh, who included another schoolboy wizard, Iggy Jones of Tyrone, in what many reckoned was the best colleges' final ever played.

Purcell, Mangan and Frank Stockwell had grown up together and played in famous Tuam street leagues but had gone their separate ways at secondary school, Purcell moving to St Jarlath's and Stockwell and Mangan remaining in Tuam CBS. Later Mangan moved to Dublin and played club football there for a time. Stockwell — 'Frankeen' as he was known in the west — went further, first to Dundalk where he played with Young Irelands and threw in his lot with Louth. Then he figured in the marathon (three games) with Meath in the 1949 championship and was even picked for the Leinster Railway Cup team the following winter. By then, however, he had moved to London. He played excellent football there and was on the London team that came back in October 1950 to play in the All-Ireland junior football final against Mayo and, somewhat ironically for a Galway man, suffered another defeat by the old enemy.

The following spring Frank returned to Tuam to join his father's decorating business and after a while was persuaded to take his football seriously again. Soon he appeared in the county team and it was around this time that a Cork Army officer, Billy O'Neill, threw in his lot with Galway. In addition some younger players began to appear in the maroon and white — Jack Mahon (Father Paddy's brother), Frank Evers, Gerry Kirwan, later Jackie Coyle and another Army man, Kerry-born Jack Kissane. The forces were gathering but, in a sense, the dispositions still were not right. By the time they met Mayo in 1954 they were searching for a full-back and, to outsiders, the amazing choice was Purcell. At full-back!

Perhaps the Galway selectors didn't quite believe that Sean's fitness levels were adequate to the demands of midfield where he had been playing regularly up to then; or they wanted to counter the threat of Mayo's great full-forward, Tom Langan. However, it wasn't a completely unfamiliar position for the Tuam star: Connacht had played him in the No. 3 spot a year and a half previously when Paddy Prendergast, the chosen full-back, cried-off the Railway Cup team for a semi-final against Leinster in Croke Park. Maybe this is where the Galway officials got the idea.

As it happened Tom Langan wasn't picked at full-forward by Mayo for this Connacht semi-final at Tuam Stadium. Mayo obviously decided that as the new National League champions they wouldn't require the services of Padraic Carney, 'the Flying Doctor,' who had returned to America immediately after the league final, for this game in July. Consequently they picked Langan at centre half-forward and moved Dan O'Neill from the corner to full-forward.

However, Langan did eventually wind-up at full-forward. Indeed during this game Mayo had three players in turn at full-forward — O'Neill, Langan and finally John Nallen from midfield — such was the overwhelming manner in which Purcell lorded it over the goalmouth area. He completely dominated his area with sure, confident fielding and an unerring reading of the game. His performance was the main contributory factor to Galway's shock win over the League champions and this has rightly been rated as Sean's 'greatest game' of all.

Galway eventually won the Connacht title and faced Kerry in the All-Ireland semi-final — which turned out to be an extraordinary match. Purcell was again at full-back, but Stockwell, who missed the Mayo game because of injury, was absent once more. Kerry were the defending champions having beaten Armagh in the previous year's final and played through the first half like champions, while Galway were obviously afflicted by Croke Park nerves, so the half-time score was 2-4 to 0-2 for Kerry.

In the second half Galway staged a remarkable recovery. First they moved Cork-born Billy O'Neill to midfield and soon brought Frank Evers also from the half-forward line to join him and the result was Galway taking over in the middle. That second half was nearly as one-sided in Galway's favour as the first was for Kerry and the champions were allowed only two more points in the second half. Galway kept piling on the pressure and then belatedly — too late many of us thought — moved Purcell out from full-back where he was isolated because of Galway's attacking tactics at the other end of the field. The real comeback came a bit too late and Kerry eventually won it by a goal.

Although initially disappointed Galway saw hope in this display, but they still had to wait some time for fulfilment. They had an undistinguished League campaign that winter and in 1955 they were shocked in the first round of the championship by Roscommon who won fairly easily in Castlebar.

It all came together in 1956. By now Gerry Daly had taken over at full-back, the veteran Tom 'Pook' Dillon had moved from centre half to left full-back and Jack Mahon had taken over the No. 6 jersey. The teenager Mattie McDonagh had come in to partner Frank Evers at midfield. Purcell was established at centre half-forward and Stockwell back again as full-forward. The combination between Purcell and Stockwell was so finely-tuned that they were able, almost, to read each other's thoughts and their team-work soon earned them the label 'The Terrible Twins' not just because only a few days separated them in their birthdays, but because of the devastation they inflicted on opposing defences. Purcell was my idea of the best all-round footballer and Stockwell had a very deceptive, jinking run that upset many backs. They were a great team together and they took it upon themselves so often to switch and swop places with great effect during important stages of matches. The third Tuam Star, Jack Mangan, had been chosen as the captain in a ballot by the panel members and this very experienced goalkeeper had a very big influence on the team, especially on the younger players. Two of the county's former most celebrated players, John Dunne and Brendan Nestor were named as joint managers — although I don't really remember any official being called a manager in those days (coaches perhaps) and Billy O'Neill, the left half-forward, was the physical trainer.

The old rivals Mayo provided the first round opposition and Galway hammered a team that was in the final throes of break-up, but still had the experienced Prendergast, Flanagan and Langan in the ranks. Galway's organised preparations paid off handsomely with a 17-point win at Castlebar. An early fright against Roscommon was overcome and the semi-final at Tuam was won by ten points with Purcell and Stockwell in superb form and then it was Sligo in the provincial final. In that match the Galway team played with utter fluency. Inspired by Purcell and with the attack flowing smoothly around his leadership they won by 13 points.

The All-Ireland semi-final brought them up against Tyrone, who had won the Ulster title for the first time. Galway were very hotly favoured for a game that saw the introduction of the 21-year-old Jackie Coyle on the half-forward line when Tom McHugh was injured. It was a very low-scoring game — not a goal between them — and Tyrone had obviously studied Galway very closely: their defence, marshalled by the late Jim Devlin, whose brother Eddie was on the half-forward line, gave the Galway forwards very little room. Still the Connacht champions were that bit more experienced and they won narrowly 0-8 to 0-6.

Within hours of that semi-final the GAA announced that both of that year's All-Ireland finals were postponed because of the outbreak of polio in Cork, the county that had teams in the two finals. The football went back to the first Sunday of October, but that didn't put a damper on Galway's ambitions. Cork had beaten Kildare in the semi-final — that, by the way, is still the last Leinster title for Kildare — but their path to the final had been plagued by an inordinate tally of wides in each game even though they had some very talented forwards like Neilly Duggan, Denis 'Toots' Kelleher, Johnny Creedon and Niall Fitzgerald. In the drawn Munster final against Kerry, for example, they kicked 26 wides and shot 21 when they beat Kildare. So the great irony of the All-Ireland final for the Munster champions was the fact that they got their shooting right — scoring 3-7 — but still lost! Against Galway they had only eight wides (to Galway's ten) yet they were beaten by a Galway team that was inspired.

So many of them played so well, but it was 'The Terrible Twins' who made it a miserable day for Cork. Purcell was scintillating and the attack worked beautifully around him, Stockwell was the ideal 'roving full-forward' as he roamed way out from the 'square' to forage hungrily and team-up perfectly with Purcell and he wound-up the final with a personal tally of two goals and five points — an 11–point total that remains the record for 60-minute finals.

It was Galway's first championship since 1938 so there were huge celebrations and the hopes were more than high for a prolonged continuance of their reign. They looked very good during the National League campaign, which began a fortnight later, despite a fright against Roscommon in the opening tie at Castlerea. They qualified for the semi-finals where they faced Tyrone again and they had to come back from a seven-point first-half deficit to win by two points, thanks mainly to Sean Purcell's contribution of 1-7 to Galway's tally of 1-10. In the final they overcame Kerry and there was a trip to New York — a prize a lot rarer then than in current times of trans-Atlantic tripping — at stake for a St Brendan Cup final in October. Galway were back to their sparkling best with Jack Mahon supreme at centre half-back and the 'Twins' in dazzling form again, switching in and out, and combining with a typical piece of wizardy and inter-passing to set-up

Stockwell for the decisive, and only, goal of the game five minutes from the end.

Now for the championship. Roscommon and Leitrim were beaten in the West and it was Cork in the All-Ireland semi-final. Then Fate intervened in Galway's ambitions in a most extraordinary and coincidental fashion. Eric Ryan, one of the Cork midfielders, equalised in the twenty-fifth minute of the second half and three minutes later kicked a winning point from a 25-yard free out on the Hogan stand side (2-4 to 0-9).

The remarkable coincidence was that 12 months later the same thing happened and, once more, deprived Galway of a place in the All-Ireland final. Just on the stroke of the sixtieth minute Dublin were awarded a free for a foul on Kevin Heffernan and as Ollie Freaney stepped up to take it he was told by Antrim referee Liam Friel that it would be the last kick of the match. Score direct or else … Ollie, who earlier had kicked two frees wide, drove the ball over the bar and Galway were out. Again!

There were many Galway supporters who to this day are convinced that their team in the 1950s was good enough to win those three championships, but ended up with only one. Whether they are right or not is a matter of opinion, but they certainly could have.

* * *

When Dublin won the championship in 1958 it ended a long period of drought for the county — a period that was traumatic in many ways, not just because of the absence of the All-Ireland title for 16 years. In the interval between 1942 and 1958 there had been dramatic changes in the Dublin football scene and, to a lesser extent, in hurling also. St Vincent's had arrived as a very formidable force in Dublin football first, and then hurling and they were determined to see changes wrought on the county teams which had for generations been peopled by country players living in Dublin with some Dublin players included.

Very often Dublin teams were made up of a combination of country players, particularly in hurling. In 1917 there wasn't one Dublin native on the team that won the All-Ireland hurling championship, Jim Byrne was the only Dublin-born player on the 1938 team and in 1942 the last football team to win the football title before the emergence of St

Vincent's included Caleb Crone (Cork), Paddy Henry (Sligo) and Joe Fitzgerald (Kerry). One reason for the preponderance of country players was the difficulty in travelling compared with nowadays when almost everyone owns a car. Additionally, it was only in 1955 that change of rule allowed players living outside their own counties to declare for their home club; up to then they had to play with clubs in the county where they were residing. Consequently there were several very powerful clubs in Dublin composed mostly of players from the provinces who couldn't go home on Sundays, as is now possible, to play for the home club. Geraldines was known as the 'Kerry' club, Clan na Gael at one time the 'teachers' club, and Sean McDermott's had players from several counties. These, along with Faughs and Young Irelands in hurling, dominated Dublin Gaelic games to a great extent, but sadly some of them like Geraldines and McDermott's are no longer in existence. One reason they declined was the desire of so many of their members to assist their home clubs, However, they also suffered from their failure to develop youth sections for juveniles and minors as they catered mostly for adult teams.

As I wrote in an earlier chapter the St Vincent's club, which had been founded in 1931, adopted a club policy from 1947 onwards that membership of the club would be available only to those born in Dublin or players eligible to play minor for the club although born outside Dublin. As club members from that period will tell you, that became known as the St Vincent's 'sinn fein' and as the club became stronger and stronger — it won its first senior football title in 1949 and first hurling in 1953 — it began to exert a greater influence on the affairs of the GAA in Dublin. Its members, especially representatives on the county board and on Dublin selection committees, pressed more and more for better recognition for Dublin-born players on the county team.

Once Vincent's became established as a new football force their existence created a new rivalry in the county between the city and country teams, as it were. It was the 'city slickers' versus 'the culchies' and it led to some mighty battles between Vincent's on the one hand and clubs like Garda, Sean McDermott's and Westerns on the other. And as they became more powerful, after winning the long yearned for first county championship, their players dominated Dublin

James O'Regan, James Hehir, Ambrose Power and Steven Clune with Clare's
All-Ireland Hurling trophy, 1914.

O'Connell School, winner of Dublin colleges' Junior Hurling Cup, 1936.
Michael O'Hehir is in front row, 2nd from left.

The Clare Team, 1914 All-Ireland final winners. Michael's father, Jim, sits at front right.

*Jo Foley, Seamus Kerr and Michael O'Hehir in the All-Hallows
College production of* Oedipus, *Easter 1935.*

Michael crossing O'Connell St bridge just two days after doing his broadcasting test in Croke Park in 1938.

Broadcasting at the Galway Races with his father, Jim, in the background.

An enthusiastic 18-year-old.

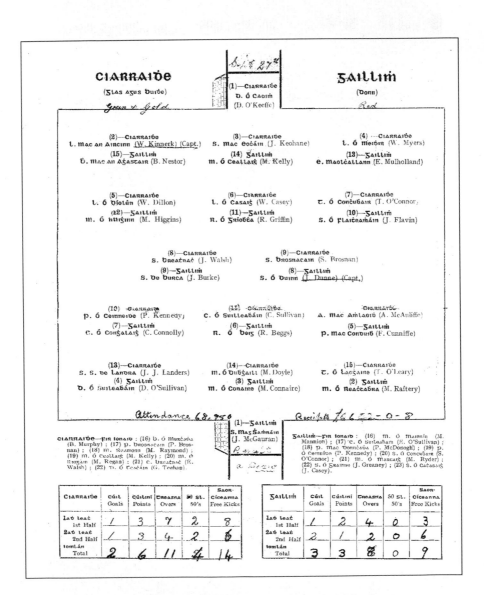

Player positions for the 1938 All-Ireland final.

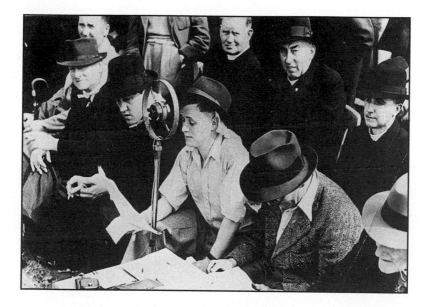

Broadcasting from Thurles in the early 1940s with plenty of clerical support.

Broadcasting from the roof of Down Royal Racecourse, 1946.

*With Kerry and Cavan players on arrival in New York 9 September 1947
for the Polo Grounds final.*

*Mayor O'Dwyer throws in the ball at the start of
the Polo Grounds Final, 1947.*

teams because their members were now ambitious to achieve an All-Ireland championship for the county especially with all-Dublin teams.

Very often Dublin teams introduced country-born players to inter-county hurling or football on the strength of the players' form with Dublin clubs. These players usually became established on the county scene during the National Leagues, but by the time the championships came along the following summer they would be persuaded by their native counties to throw in their lot with the home county. This caused much upset in Dublin circles, especially with the county's selectors who had brought these players to the forefront in the first place. The selectors and Dublin-born team-mates of these players felt they were being deserted at a time when Dublin needed these players most: at championship time. So it wasn't surprising that there was a growing feeling among Dublin-born players and officials, prompted to a large extent by the increasingly successful St Vincent's, that Dublin teams should be for Dubliners. Although this 'policy' was never formally accepted by Dublin at a county convention it became the accepted practice that Dublin teams consisted of Dubliners or those who were reared in Dublin from an early age. Two best-known examples in the latter category were Denis Mahony, born in Cork, and Des Ferguson, born in Down, who were both brought up in Dublin and went to primary school in the city. In hurling there were some prime exceptions to this — a group of hurlers who gave their first allegiance to Dublin no matter how persuasive the invitations from their native counties. Jim Prior (1952) and Paddy Croke (1961), both from Tipperary, were unswerving in their loyalty to Dublin.

Having said all that it should be stressed that the St Vincent's 'sinn fein' was never as completely restrictive as some people now seem to think and membership from the early days was also available to applicants 'who were ordinarily resident in the parishes of Marino, Fairview and Clontarf.' In the 1940s two prominent playing members were Donie McGrath, a Cork man in goal, and Tyrone-born Frank Harte in midfield and, of course, in latter times Ciaran Barr, the Antrim hurler, transferred from O'Donovan Rossa in Belfast to St Vincent's.

During the early 1950s Dublin teams changed radically, especially in football, and their fortunes took a turn for the better. In 1952 the team reached the National Football League home final but lost to Cork only by a single point. The following year they went all the way with a team that was extraordinary in its selection of 14 St Vincent's players and Dubliner Tony O'Grady from the Air Corps club in goal. That side won the first League title for Dublin when they beat Cavan in the final.

The increasing success of this Dublin team had two effects: it brought thousands of Dubliners out in support of the side — people who were more accustomed to attending soccer games and had never been attracted to Gaelic games by teams that contained so many country-born players — and it caused a depth of feeling among the country people living in Dublin who now flocked to the matches to see Vincents and Dublin beaten. Which, of course, was the city versus country thing again.

This intense rivalry became all the more pronounced in 1955. Despite the National League success — and they did it again in 1955 when they annihilated Meath in the final in May — Dublin hearts were set on the championship as is the ambition of every county player. Not only had the county not won the All-Ireland title since 1942 they hadn't captured the Leinster championship in the same period. They were thwarted in the early 1950s, but became champions of the province again in 1955 with victories over Carlow (12 points), Offaly (3 points) and Meath (again a huge winning margin: 5-12 to 0-7) before meeting Mayo in the All-Ireland semi-final.

The team was gathering great support as it went along: over 48,000 saw the Leinster final and the game against Mayo attracted 60,595 compared with 41,278 at the Kerry-Cavan semi-final a week earlier. Both semi-finals ended in draws and, in a unique football programme, the two replays were staged on the same day. Mayo still had some of their outstanding players who had won the two titles a few years before — Paddy Prendergast, Sean and Mick Flanagan, Eamonn Mongey, Peter Solan and Tom Langan. The fact that some of the Mayo players lived and worked in Dublin made the rivalry all the keener. It was a ding-dong, hectic battle before Dublin scraped through by a single point (1-8 to 1-7).

Kerry easily beat Cavan in their replay and the counties were set for their first meeting in a final since 1924. Three decades earlier they had been frequent rivals, but this was very, very different.

No final in modern times had such a build-up of excitement — and, indeed, tension. It was the ultimate 'country versus city' clash: Kerry the traditionally strong football super-power still leading the championship lists decade after decade with 17 titles; Dublin, the recently-crowned new National League winners, having won their first league only two years before, and representing a county that lay in second place with 15 championships, but without one now for 13 years. Not only were Kerry itching to get compensation for their disappointment the previous year when beaten by Meath, they couldn't wait to get at Dublin, these new upstarts — brash and confident — in the football world.

Kerry played their football as Kerry teams had done so successfully for many generations: with style and strength, relying on superb fielding and quick, incisive kicking to deliver the ball to shrewd, intelligent and opportunistic forwards who, as usual, had a marvellous ability to pick off long-range points. The new Dublin team, represented by those born or reared in the capital city and its surrounds, moved the ball differently with short-passing movements, precise combination and with full-forward Kevin Heffernan roaming far out from the goalmouth and striking-up a menacing brand of team-work with centre half Ollie Freaney — an arrangement which had devastated Meath twice already that summer.

Dublin had been so impressive in Leinster, and then in overcoming Mayo in the replayed semi-final, that they were being widely fancied for the final — but the level of optimism that swept the capital was hardly justified. There were doubts expressed even outside Dublin about the Kerry defence and their confrontation with the cohesive Dublin forwards. Particularly there were questions about the ability (and mobility) of their full-back Ned Roche to cope with Kevin Heffernan who had roamed out near midfield in the semi-final — and had taken Paddy Prendergast with him everywhere he went. But to the astonishment of all Dubliners the Kerry backs were magnificent. Their trainer, Dr Eamonn O'Sullivan, and the selectors had done their homework and worked-out a defensive strategy of close policing on the Dubs' forwards. Army officer Roche, in particular, was very defiant and John Cronin, the centre half, was inflexible and outcaught everyone. In addition, the two corner backs, Jerome O'Shea and Micksey Palmer closed off avenues to goal when Dublin came on the attack, although it was noticeable that Heffernan didn't rove out nearly as far as in other games.

Dublin missed a lot of chances early on and by half-time Kerry were two points ahead before a record crowd of 87,102 and they went four up soon after the resumption. There was only one goal in it — ironically scored by Dublin when Ollie Freaney's 14-yard free was booted straight through the packed goalmouth into the net. But it was too late to save the Dubs — it came in the 56th minute.

The rejoicing in Kerry possibly surpassed anything that had gone before: they felt they had taught the 'upstarts' from Dublin a lesson and the gloom in Dublin was very deep indeed. Dublin recovered fairly quickly though and were good enough to reach the semi-final of the National League the following spring but lost in a replay to Cork.

In the meantime the word about the 1955 All-Ireland being one of the greatest in latter times had spread to America. There was no possibility of seeing the game live, or even on video later, in those days and radio broadcasts had not started regularly. So the exiles depended on newspapers and letters sent from home in the subsequent weeks to learn all about the big games. The people in New York now decided they wanted to see Kerry and Dublin — and with the Kerry influence in the New York GAA exerted by John 'Kerry' O'Donnell and others an invitation was issued to the teams. With Central Council approval they travelled out in the first days of June — just a few days after Dublin had beaten Wicklow in the first round of the Leinster championship. They played a 'repeat' of the All-Ireland final in the famous Polo Grounds before 25,000 and Dublin won this one by 14 points. New York officials were quoted as saying it 'was the greatest game of Gaelic football played anywhere.' The following Sunday they were in Gaelic Park to play New York's first and second teams, but it was a costly trip for Dublin because they came home with several injuries and, without Jim Crowley, Kevin Hefferan and Marcus Wilson they lost a championship match to Wexford in Carlow two weeks later.

In 1957 they were beaten in the Leinster final by Louth, but they regrouped for the National League that began later that year. Several of the stalwarts of the early 1950s had now departed from the team — Denis Mahony, Jim Lavin, Mick Moylan and Nicky Maher — and a new side was built up which captured the league title with a win over Kildare in the final. New names appeared — Joe and John Timmons, Sean 'Yank' Murray and Paddy Farnan among them — and they had a big victory over Meath in the first round of the 1958 championship.

Carlow, Louth and Galway were the next victims — Ollie Freaney's late pointed free being the semi-final winner — and they faced a final against Derry, who had won their first Ulster title only two months before and on a dreadful day of wind and rain had shocked Kerry in the All-Ireland semi-final.

However, there was to be no surprise in the final. Dublin were well forewarned and even though Derry's outstanding midfielder Jim McKeever emphasised once again what a great player he was, it was Dublin who won in the end. Derry produced an all-round excellent display of wonderful fielding but Dublin's combination was superior with their forwards in superb form. The Dubs led by four points at half-time, but wound-up six-point winners. So the Sam Maguire Cup rested in Dublin at long last — and a 'Dublin' Dublin team had at long last achieved its ambition!

6

The Sizzling Sixties

From the time Kerry won their first All-Ireland football championship in 1903 the county never went through a decade without some success — although that hasn't been their fate in the first half of the 1990s and, indeed, up to and including 1996 they have failed even to get to the final. But those hard times were still to come and in the 1960s they captured two titles. That decade, though, really belonged to Galway and Down, who between them won six of the ten championships, three apiece. Of course, 1960 was a year that truly goes down in history: Down's first appearance in the All-Ireland final, their first triumph and the first time for the Sam Maguire Cup to be carried across the Border into the Six Counties. In hurling, Tipperary were fabulously successful and got four All-Ireland championships as well as five National Leagues — a string of successes that got them branded as hurling's 'League specialists' as Mayo had been with football in the 1930s.

In latter years we have become accustomed to Ulster teams winning the football championship or at least being very strong contenders. But up to the 1950s there had only been Cavan to challenge seriously for the title. Monaghan had one try (1930) as did Armagh (1953) and Derry (1958) and, of course, Antrim in 1911 and 1912. Not only had Down not been seriously considered, they often failed to get past the first round and appeared in only two Ulster finals (1940 and 1942) before the 1950s.

But all that was about to change in the second half of the 1950s. In 1950 itself Down got past the first round, but lost to Armagh. However, for the next seven years they failed to surmount the first hurdle in the championship until 1958. Then they beat Donegal and Tyrone before losing to Derry in the county's first provincial final in 16 years. Things had been so bad at one stage that Maurice Hayes, their county secretary in this period, once stated: 'I remember being at a match in Lurgan in which first of all we could hardly get a team and from which the selectors had disappeared before the team took the field.'

Many people have given great credit to Maurice Hayes as one of those who contributed inordinately to bringing Down out of the shadows. A native of Downpatrick, his father was from Waterford and his mother from Listowel and Maurice had lived for a time during childhood in Co. Waterford. Here he had developed a passionate love for hurling and he was one of those who founded the Downpatrick hurling club in the mid-1940s. He was devoted to all things Gaelic — the language and the games — and he was elected assistant secretary of the Down Board in 1948 and then succeeded Peadar Barry as secretary seven years later. He also served as Down's representative on the Central Council of the GAA from 1955 for nine years. In latter times he was a very prominent member of the Northern Ireland Civil Service and was ombudsman in the North for some years.

When Down eventually got to the top of the football ladder their captain was Kevin Mussen, who was nearing the end of his long career and had played with solid dedication along with such people as George Lavery, Jarlath Carey, Kieran Denvir and Paddy Doherty throughout the lean years. They were still there (fortunately) when the good times arrived: I remember Kevin once telling me that 'no one could praise Maurice Hayes too much for planning all of this.' He added: 'To my way of thinking the All-Ireland was Maurice's dream, he had a notion I think away about 1956 that Down could win an All-Ireland.' Hayes himself recalling that black day in Lurgan revealed: 'There were a few of us had got so fed up at that stage that we decided we would make this a team people would want to play for and follow.'

Among his able helpers were Barney Carr, himself a former great Down player, Dr Martin Walsh, Danny Flynn, George Tinnelly, who was county chairman for nearly 20 years up to 1966, and T.P. Murphy, who was assistant secretary for several years before succeeding Hayes in 1965. Maurice Hayes has said: 'The rest of the county thought we were on a hiding to nothing and were quite willing to let us make fools of ourselves.'

Which of course, they didn't. It was a long struggle, but eventually they succeeded in putting together a more formidable team than Down ever fielded. The schools in the county, particularly the two in Newry

— St Colman's College (Violet Hill) and the Abbey CBS — made a huge contribution because they were producing some splendid young footballers at that time like James and Dan McCartan (Colman's), Kevin and Sean O'Neill from the Abbey.

There were other factors, like the establishment of an all-county senior football league and the decision to seek games against opposition — any opposition — outside the province of Ulster, and all of these contributed in some small way to the coming together of the best talent in the county — some very skilful and accomplished talent that was nurtured and coached with care and perseverence. The selectors and administrators like Hayes kept on pounding out the message that it would take at least five years and that patience and persistence were needed.

The players responded enthusiastically, both the young ones and those with long service, and soon there were signs that Down could emerge as a new force in football. By 1958 they were able to get past the first round of the championship for the first time in eight years beating Donegal and Tyrone before losing the provincial final to the Derry team that was good enough to go ahead and reach the All-Ireland final. So 1959 opened with lots of promise. A selection committee of three was appointed by the county board — Maurice Hayes, Barney Carr and Brian Denvir. Carr was then named as manager and Danny Flynn, a teacher at Castlewellan school, was chosen as the trainer. Under this management team's guidance Down set a precedent by launching a programme of winter training and by 1960, the year of their breakthrough, they were indulging in a set programme of indoor training at Castlewellan from late January and moving outdoors to Newcastle or some other venue by the end of March.

More importantly, they were trendsetters in being the first team put through twice weekly training sessions. They were brought together every Tuesday and Thursday evening from early in the year and this continued right through the playing season — something that is commonplace nowadays even with the lowliest of county teams but in the late 1950s was unheard of even by the counties that would eventually get to the All-Ireland series. By August and September, when they began appearing in All-Ireland semi-finals, this training would be stepped-up to include a match and training again on Saturdays.

And it all paid off. In Ulster the McKenna Cup competition is a championship warm-up welcomed by the counties and Down used it very profitably in 1959. Their first victory was in April over Donegal, then Derry and a win in the final over Monaghan, which was Down's first major trophy victory since the Lagan Cup success in 1948. Eight days earlier the team had played at Wembley Stadium against Galway in the second of what was the London County Board's Whit tournaments which ran with great success until the mid-Seventies. This was a game that forced many football fans to sit up and take notice of these 'johnny-come-latelys' from Ulster. A crowd of 32,000 people including hundreds of Down fans attended the game. Some of these had travelled over with the team on a plane specially chartered in another pioneering move by the county board. It was a real thriller with Down winning 3-9 to 4-4, Patsy O'Hagan (two) and Sean O'Neill getting the goals.

At this time I hadn't seen a great deal of Down football; in fact, I think I did a commentary in Newry on one of their matches in the Lagan Cup competition, which doubled as the first division of the National League in those days. Soon, though, I was to get a very good look at them in Croke Park. They began their championship campaign in June with a win over Antrim and then were invited to Dublin to play Dublin, the reigning All-Ireland champions, in a tournament game in aid of the St Vincent's club grounds. No doubt the influence of Liam Ferguson, a native of Down and Des's father, who was prominent on the club committee had a lot to do with Down being asked to Dublin, but the invitation would have been clinched by the quickly growing reputation the Down team was getting. They repaid the Vincent's invitation with another spectacular display, using all the spaces of the big Croke Park pitch on this their first visit. Over 9,000 turned up for this tournament and they were treated to great football with Dublin getting a draw only with a late goal.

Down then had a setback when held to a draw by Tyrone in the championship, but they won the replay easily and next came the Ulster final against Cavan, the county that had traditionally lorded it in the north. But Cavan were hammered by 15 points. When it came to the All-Ireland semi-final Galway had obviously learned from Wembley and inspired by Sean Purcell and Frank Evers the Connacht champions made their experience pay-off to reach the final. But Down were still on course with the five-year plan drawn up mainly by Hayes and Carr in 1956.

It didn't take long for Down to bounce back. I didn't see them over that winter, but heard glowing reports of their National League performances — that was in Division 1 or the Lagan Cup as it was known then — and they demolished Derry in the final of the division in March. Then they came to Croke Park and beat Kerry, who were the All-Ireland and National League champions the previous year, in the semi-final. In an all-Ulster final they met Cavan and it drew a record crowd for a National League final to Croke Park of 49,451. It was a very exciting match even though it didn't produce a goal (0-12 to 0-9), but it gave Down their first trophy at national level. And a huge boost to their confidence for the championship campaign they would start in five weeks time.

They romped through the earlier matches, beating Antrim and Monaghan and retained the title in Ulster with another victory over Cavan. Then came an abrupt halt to their progress. In the All-Ireland semi-final they encountered Offaly, who just a few weeks earlier had won the county's first ever Leinster championship. And I well remember the shock Down got: Offaly were 2-4 to 0-3 up at half-time. None of us had expected that, but certainly not the buoyant Ulster champions. However, Down showed us the stern stuff they were made of when they staged a magnificent comeback after the interval. Paddy Doherty goaled from a penalty and kicked five points and, at the end, it was Offaly's Harry Donnelly who equalised for Offaly from a free to force a replay.

The replay in September saw Offaly go into an early lead, but when downpours of rain arrived Down changed their close-passing tactics and indulged in long deliveries which paid dividends against the previously stubborn Offaly defence. Consequently Down qualified for their first ever All-Ireland final. And what a mouth-watering prospect that held out for us: Down, the lately emergent, once 'weak' county, facing up to the mighty Kerry, who then led the roll of championship honour with 19 titles. And the Sam Maguire Cup never having crossed over the border! We wondered how Down would handle the team that had so much tradition behind them apart from being the defending champions. I was certainly one of those who felt that the meeting in the National League earlier mightn't have too much relevance for the simple reason that we all knew that nothing mattered to Kerry more than the championship.

Many years afterwards Sean O'Neill, the young right half-forward of 1960, told me that they went to Croke Park without being too concerned about Kerry because they had supreme confidence in their own ability. He added: 'You know athletes know when they have quality. As a team we knew we had the qualities necessary to win an All-Ireland final. We had great respect for Kerry, but we did not fear them. As the game developed we had a good start, the first half went our way and the good start gave us confidence.'

Once again Down helped smash attendance records as a crowd of 87,768 turned up for this final — those, of course, the days when all-ticket matches were unheard of in this country and people didn't mind the discomfort of being squeezed into the terraces at the two ends and under the Cusack Stand. Indeed, I can still visualise the way the crowds on the Hill, particularly, used sway and heave because of the absence in those days of as many crush barriers as there are nowadays on terraces.

Down were the first to score in the final, but the first half didn't produce a goal as the Ulster champions led 0-7 to 0-5 at half-time. At centre half-forward James McCartan was a colossus. McCartan and his brother Dan were sons of Brian, who had the reputation of being a 'hardy' footballer with Down in his young days. James remembers the journey home by car from the 1959 semi-final defeat and being 'scolded' by his father. When the car arrived in the yard in Doneycloney James vowed 'Daddy, we'll win it next year if I have to steal it.' And no one did more to make sure Down would win than Big James. Eleven minutes into the second half he lobbed in a centre from about 40 yards and Kerry's great goalkeeper, Johnny Culloty, had the awful misfortune to mishandle his catch and it slipped in over his head to the net. James was involved again a minute later in a passing movement with his cousin Sean O'Neill who sent the ball on to Paddy Doherty. Paddy was fouled in the 'square' and he belted the resultant penalty to the net. After that there was no stopping Down and they won 2-10 to 0-8.

Throughout my broadcasting career there have been certain things that have remained in the mind. One of these is the scene after Down won that first All-Ireland. I shall never forget the atmosphere in Croke

Park when their captain, Kevin Mussen, held the Sam Maguire Cup high. The whole of Croke Park — indeed the whole of Dublin and Ireland — seemed to erupt with enthusiasm and roaring as a tribute to the men of Down for coming south to win the All-Ireland. Of course, in recent years there have been impressive scenes of huge jubilation when teams win the championship — most notably when Clare and Dublin won the 1995 finals and when Wexford triumphed in 1996. But in 1960 there was no such thing as opening gates to allow access from Hill 16 — there were no gates, just wire fences then — and where the Down people came from I don't know: they got onto the pitch anyhow and with over 20,000 more spectators at the final in 1960 than there could be 35 or 36 years later you can just imagine the massive flood of people out onto the pitch. It got to the stage that Maurice Hayes, the county secretary, whispered to Kevin Mussen 'we're not going down there' and the team attempted to 'escape' into the back of the Hogan Stand. But the dressing-rooms at that time were under the Cusack Stand and the players had to battle their way over the field. To this day many of them will tell you that was the roughest part of the afternoon!

The reaction to Down's triumph was remarkable — as might be expected with the Sam Maguire Cup going over the border for the first time. On the journey home on the Monday evening they encountered large crowds all along the way welcoming them: a huge throng was out in Drogheda, another in Dundalk at the courthouse and it was all hours in the morning by the time they reached Newcastle after travelling through Newry, Hilltown — Kevin Mussen's home village — and Castlewellan where they were greeted by a torchlight procession. One important aspect of their win was the delight of their Protestant neighbours at their victory. There was no need to go looking for tickets for the terraces in those days and many of them had been at the semi-final. (In that era semi-final tickets for all parts of the stadium were freely available not only from Croke Park, but also from Clerys and Elverys.)

Kevin Mussen tells the story of the morning after the team's victory over Cavan in the National League final earlier in the year. The local postman in Hilltown was a recognised Orangeman and also a member of the B Specials, an auxiliary police force who didn't endear themselves to the Catholic and Nationalist community. When this gentleman called on that Monday morning to deliver the Mussen mail he spied the League trophy which Kevin had brought home the previous evening. His eyes lit up and turning to Kevin's mother he declared with as much passion as any Down supporter had shown the previous day in Croke Park: 'Christ, we took it off the friggers!' Orangeman or not, it was still a case of 'them and us.' Not only that, but the Down team some time after the All-Ireland final were invited to pay an official visit to Belfast City Hall for a civic reception by the then mayor, Alderman William Geddes. That was a splendid occasion and, when the formalities were over, the evening developed into a very lively singsong with none singing the 'Mountains of Mourne' and 'The Star of the County Down' more lustily than the Unionist councillors despite the protesting Paisleyite supporters shouting their anger outside.

How times had changed by 1994 when another generation of Down sportsmen brought the Sam Maguire to the North. Then a motion to invite that team to the Civic Hall was defeated by the majority of Unionist councillors and within a month or so the much welcomed, but impermanent, ceasefire had come to the North! Down got down to the business of the National League at the end of October, a few weeks after they had easily beaten the visiting New York team in the St Brendan Cup final at Croke Park. But the following March they lost their Division 1 title (and the Lagan Cup) when beaten by Derry in the Lagan Cup final at Casement Park. As it happened the rest from the intense competition of the latter stages of the league was probably a benefit to them when they came to defend their championships.

Obviously the rest did them all the good in the world. When it came to May they showed just how refreshed they were by hammering Monaghan in the McKenna Cup final and six days later produced a sparkling display at Wembley Stadium to beat Kerry easily. Then it was on to the championship and victories over Fermanagh, Derry (after a fright) and Armagh (by just a goal) sent them back to Croke Park and yet another confrontation with Kerry. This All-Ireland semi-final, setting a crowd record (71,573) for this stage of the championship, confirmed Down's position of never failing to Kerry in the championship — a stance that has been maintained to this day after meeting in two finals and two semi-finals. They got the ideal start with a goal by Sean O'Neill in the very first minute and so were on the way to yet another win over Kerry.

I can still remember looking out across Croke Park from the still relatively new commentary box — the Hogan Stand was just over two years old — at the extraordinary spectacle the stadium presented for the final between Down and Offaly. A unique occasion in many ways, not least because the opponents were counties away down the pecking order — Down with that one All-Ireland title from the previous year and Offaly appearing in the final for the very first time. Talk about not being rich in tradition; there wasn't an ounce of it between the two of them! Yet, the match attracted the greatest gathering of spectators to attend any sporting event in this country — and maybe it was the novelty of the pairing that brought 90,566 to Croke Park on that remarkable day.

Down were certainly called upon to demonstrate their champions' power because their resolve and nerve were put to the test severely even though they opened the scoring with a quick point in half a minute of the start. However, in the next five minutes Offaly stunned the champions with goals from Mick Casey and Peter Daly and a point from Har Donnelly. But Down were now showing their mettle and before half-time Sean O'Neill and James McCartan both had goals within the space of 90 seconds, putting Down a goal ahead at the break.

Unfortunately the second half, although a rousing battle, wasn't as good from the football point of view as the first. The teams had exhausted their ability to score goals with five in the first half and the Down defence stood up magnificently to most Offaly assaults in the second to ensure that the Ulster side would edge through by a single point. Offaly felt hard done by in that second half when they believed that wing forward Tommy Greene should have been awarded a penalty after being pulled down in the goal area. But it wasn't to be.

The celebrations went on again for a long time, but they didn't weaken Down's commitment to the National League that started in October. They did so well that the following May, they faced Dublin in the final. During the winter the American Board of the GAA, a body which organised all cities outside New York across America and Canada, was recognised by the Central Council and they immediately invited the All-Ireland champions to tour the US.

The tour was arranged for May 1962 and the team and supporters were due out of Ireland just three days after the National League final in which the All-Ireland champions met Dublin. A crowd of 56,515 was the highest at a League final up to then — it has since been surpassed: in fact, just two years later when over 70,000 watched, would you believe, Dublin and Down. As they went into that 1962 final Down, needless to say, were anxious to head for America not only as All-Ireland champions, but also holding football's double. But they were rocked by Dublin, who were appearing in their first national final since winning both the league and championship in 1958. Down were behind by four points at half-time after Dublin's Mickey Whelan — yes, the manager nowadays — got the only goal of the first half. And they were still in arrears with little more than four minutes left (1-5 to 1-7) even after an early second half goal by half-back Kevin Mussen, the man who had taken the cups across the border in 1960. Now at the end Mussen was in attack, having been switched to the half-forward line, and soon he was put through by Joe Lennon for a shot that was handled on the ground by the Dublin defence. Penalty! I wouldn't have liked to have been in Sean O'Neill's shoes as he stepped up to that all-important shot, but the right half-forward cooly drove it into the net and Down were the double champions.

They got a great reception in the United States and played matches against American Board selections in Boston, Cleveland, Chicago and Philadelphia and a West Coast selection in San Francisco. I wasn't able to go on the full tour but was invited out for the games in Cleveland and Philadelphia by the president of the organising body, Mickey Cavanaugh, a Mayo man living in Philly for many years and who later returned to the hotel business in Westport. In Philadelphia I organised a day at the races for some of the party, including the Down secretary, Maurice Hayes, who were interested in the horses. As far as I remember we had an enjoyable — and successful — afternoon, but when Down left the day after their match for San Francisco I wasn't with them as I had to be in Epsom two days later for the English Derby. Some of the Down people had entrusted me with some of the Philly dollars to put on the Vincent O'Brien runner Larkspur in the classic.

That race was notable for being Vincent's first English Derby winner as Larkspur, ridden by the Australian Neville Sellwood, duly obliged at the handsome price of 22/1. Now remember by this time Down were in San Francisco and when the news came through of the great Irish win there were joyous scenes in the team's hotel. As Maurice Hayes told me some time later: 'A winner at 22/1 so we went on a spending spree.'

Oh, alas and alack! I never made it to Epsom. Sad to say, I was held up in New York and couldn't get out as scheduled because of the summer fog that often descends and disrupts flights. So I didn't make it across the Atlantic in time for the Derby on the Wednesday with the embarrassing sequel that when Down got home about a week later I had to confess that I hadn't got their bets down. Imagine their disappointment: a wonder, I've often thought since, that they didn't strangle me.

It was on that American tour that a former gridiron football star made a marvellous remark to James McCartan. This was a gentleman called Johnny MacMullan, who had been a noted player in his days at Notre Dame University. He had been taken to Down's match in Chicago by some Irish-American friends and afterwards was introduced to the players. When he got to the McCartan brothers he declared: 'I liked you, Dan, that long ball down the middle — but Christ, James, you're my guy: big and mean and nasty!'

When Down returned from that month-long tour in 1962 they were quickly into the defence of their titles. All went well in the games against Fermanagh and Tyrone, but they came unstuck in the Ulster final at Casement Park when Cavan exacted extreme revenge for the defeats of 1959 and 1960 by winning 3-6 to 0-5. In those days there was a commonly held belief that a trip to America by a county team as close to the championship as May or June put a jinx on the tourists and this dethronement of Down added weight to this.

Down, of course, came back the following year to retake the title from Cavan — they seemed to be taking turns about with the provincial crown in those days — but it was 1968 before they got back to the previous heights of success. By then there were several changes in the team: Eamonn McKay, George Lavery, Leo Murphy, Pat Rice, Jarlath Carey, James McCartan, Tony Hadden and P.J. McElroy had departed and the next generation had come with younger players like Danny Kelly, Brendan Sloan, Tom O'Hare, Colm McAlarney, Jimmy Milligan, Mickey Cole, Peter Rooney, John Murphy and John Purdy. They recaptured the National League in May and then began the championship campaign with a very tempestuous match against Derry in Ballinascreen. They overcame Donegal and Cavan to qualify for the All-Ireland semi-final against Galway, which they narrowly won. And once more it was an All-Ireland final against Kerry.

It looked as if Down would romp to victory when they went eight points up in eight minutes after a sensational goal in the sixth minute — a dream start. Peter Rooney's shot came back off the post and Sean O'Neill, now full-forward for the past three years, was following up quickly and alertly and booted the rebound, first time, into the Kerry net. It was 2-7 to 0-5 at half-time, but the Munster champions fought back in the second half. However, Brendan Lynch's goal from a 14-yard free came only in the last minute and too late to prevent Down winning another championship.

A few years before, the GAA had attempted to counteract the impact the 1966 World Cup soccer in England had made, principally through the influence of television, by instituting a new competition between the All-Ireland champions (replacing New York in the National League finals) and called with extreme extravagance, 'The World Championship Cup'. But then if two baseball teams from New York could play for a 'World Series' why couldn't two teams of Irishmen — placed on either side of the Atlantic — play-off for the World championship of Gaelic football? So within a few weeks Down were off to New York and they played New York at Gaelic Park where they won on the aggregate from two Sundays. Thus the county collected three trophies for 1968.

But could any of us have guessed that it would be many, many years before the county would win a major title again: 15 until their next National League and all of 23 until an All-Ireland crown!

The other team to win three All-Ireland football championships in the 1960s was Galway. Unlike Down, the county had already got its name on the roll of honour — 1956 being their fourth title — and their team went one better than Down in that they won three-in-a-row from four successive finals. Of course, both Kerry and Wexford had won four consecutive finals, but the three-in-a-row was still something of a rarity and it hadn't been achieved for all of 25 years by the time Galway did it — Kerry in 1939–1941 being the last to accomplish the feat. In the meantime Roscommon (1945), Cavan (1949), Mayo (1952) and Down (1962) all failed to add the third title, so Galway's success was a not inconsiderable accomplishment in 1964–1966. They were beaten in the 1963 final by Dublin and I often thought, then and since, that this was an even better team than in the following three years. But over 87,000 spectators saw them indulge in a dreadful wastage of possession; they had most of the play but kicked 12 wides to Dublin's four.

It was a chastening lesson for Galway, but was well learned. The process had begun, though, three years or so previously. That's when Galway won the minor championship and this successful team contained several of those who would be taking part in the senior triumphs in that three-in-a-row: Enda Colleran, Noel Tierney, Sean Cleary, Christy Tyrrell and Seamus Leydon. In addition their management team was a triumvirate with Frank Stockwell, the full-forward hero of 1956, joining the 1938 medallists, John Dunne and Brendan Nestor, in charge.

This trio had a very considerable influence on Galway's successes — in a much different way, I'd say, than the present-day managers and their selectors, whether it be a 'team' of three or five. In Galway in the 1960s their football team was chosen by a selection committee of nine and, sometimes, eleven selectors — an unheard of number nowadays and a selection committee the size of which wouldn't be tolerated anywhere these days. The three — Nestor, Dunne and Stockwell — were members of this committee which was chaired by the chairman of the Football Board, Father Paddy Mahon, and the team on the field was then under the complete control of the managerial trio. They were three different personalities, all of them outstanding footballers in their own right and in very varied ways: Dunne and Nestor from one generation and Stockwell from another. Brendan Nestor lived life to the full, was a lively companion who liked a wee drink or two, sometimes more. John Dunne was abrasive and brusque but could be very welcoming and generous when you really got to know him and he warmly greeted you on your visits to Galway. An inveterate gambler, he was as familiar to me on racecourses as he was on the football fields and, remember, both himself and Brendan had played in that Mullingar match when I did my first broadcast in 1938. Stockwell was the hero of their 1956 All-Ireland triumph and his partnership in attack with Sean Purcell was one of the outstanding features of football in the 1950s. He was as friendly a person as you could wish — totally in love with the game of football, although well-versed in most sports, and a very shrewd 'reader' of a game.

They had a very good working relationship although sometimes they differed greatly in their views during a match about what should be done — and that's when the advantage of a trio came into effect. Usually it was Stockwell who acted as the deciding factor and as the 1960s went on he became a more important influence. I remember John Donnellan once telling me that John Dunne 'was a bit of a bully in many ways, but Frank Stockwell who trained us most of the time was a great guy to motivate people.'

I often visited the Galway players in training — mostly when I'd be in Galway for the races or if I was spending a few days in Mayo I'd drive over to Tuam Stadium. They were a very happy bunch, more like a big family and in various groups they socialised together outside of football. One of the notable features of their training sessions was that they were in no hurry to rush away from the stadium after a session. In fact when it was put to them at the outset of their campaigning about eating arrangements after training they declined to repair to a hotel for a meal, as most teams did even then, preferring to stay around Tuam Stadium to partake of sandwiches and milk organised by local officials in a spare dressing-room. The reason: they preferred the 'craic' and banter that this informal meal generated. They had an extraordinary capacity for drinking milk; in fact, as far as I can recall only two or three of them took a beer and then not always during the championship.

Later in their reign they were in New York for a National League final, which I broadcast. A trip to the World's Fair, then being held in New York, was organised by the Coca Cola company at the behest of the local bottlers of that soft drink in Tuam. During the visit to the fair in Flushing Meadows the team and officials were entertained at a snazzy restaurant and Seán Ó Siocháin, the GAA's director general, drew the attention of some New York-based Galwaymen who had accompanied them to what might happen when a cocktail waiter went around the party to take a drinks order. 'Watch the amount of milk these fellows'll order,' says Ó Siocháin, 'Since travelling out with them I can't get over all the milk they drink.' And sure enough the bulk of the order the waiter took away was for glasses of milk — at a time when these players were welcome to order any drink under the sun.' Would it happen with any bunch of players nowadays, I wonder?

In May 1964 Galway were in London for the annual tournament the local county board organised at Wembley Stadium. That competition started in 1958 and a few years later the still-young Independent Television channel would cover a portion of the hurling match for their Saturday afternoon *World of Sport* programme. The installation of an outside broadcast unit at the stadium, even for 15 minutes coverage of the game, enabled RTE to transmit the two matches live to Ireland. So I was with them when they beat Dublin in a thriller just six days after Dublin, the All-Ireland champions, had hammered Down in the home final of the National League.

That was a tremendous boost for Galway and revenge for the previous year's All-Ireland final defeat. It set them up for the championship. They got something of a fright in the first game against Sligo, but then walloped Mayo to qualify for the All-Ireland semi-final. There they had a narrow win over a Meath team that wasted many chances, particularly from their usually accurate free-taker Jimmy Walsh, who amazed us all by missing several frees. The Leinster champions had no one to blame, really, but their own forwards. However, they were very angry afterwards with Seamus Garvey, a Kerry-born Garda stationed in Cork who was the referee. They were so upset by some of Seamus' decisions that the following November, when they had qualified for the final of a Grounds' Tournament by beating Cork, they strenuously objected to Garvey being appointed for the final against Galway. Needless to say the Central Council executive, which appointed the referees in those days, would not take Garvey off the match and Meath withdrew from the final. Consequently Dublin, who had lost to Meath in the Leinster final, were invited to play Galway in the semi-final — the fact that they did angered Meath even more, as I recall. It's fairly certain you wouldn't see such a breaking of ranks in Leinster today even though Meath and Dublin are still intense rivals.

In the All-Ireland final of 1964 Galway's opponents were Kerry, the traditional lords of football, but the Connacht champions had a fairly convincing win even though they didn't score a goal (0-15 to 0-10) over a team that included such legendary Kingdom footballers as Mick O'Dwyer, Mick O'Connell and Tom Long. The strange thing about that goal-less final is that Galway, in their four successive finals, obtained only one goal and that was in the last of the four against Meath in 1966. Another feature of that Galway triumph was that they didn't have need for a substitute — and that's something only three other teams (Meath, 1967; Kerry, 1969 and Dublin, 1974) have done in the 32 years (1965–1996) since then. What's more, in their three winning finals Galway called on only two subs — Mick Reynolds in 1965 and John Donnellan in 1966.

Donnellan was the victorious captain in 1964 but his moment of triumph was overshadowed by the tragedy of his father's death during the final. Mick Donnellan, a former great county player, had collapsed in the lower deck of the Hogan Stand and despite medical attention sadly passed away before seeing his son take the Sam Maguire Cup. John and Enda Colleran, the right full-back who would be captain for the next two years, had actually noticed a commotion in the stand during the second half and they came to the conclusion that a row or something had broken out. It was only after crossing the field with the cup and entering a very gloomy Cusack Stand dressing-room that John was told his father had passed away.

It so happened that Galway's celebrations were considerably muted in the few days following the final. By terrible coincidence another former great player and team-mate of Mick Donnellan, Mick Higgins, died in Galway city on the evening of the final having watched the match on television during the afternoon.

Within eight months Kerry got a chance of avenging their All-Ireland final defeat. The teams met in the home final of the 1964–'65 National League and there was added interest in this clash because the winners would qualify for a trip to New York the following month for the final proper.

The final was a controversial one: Kerry led three times against the All-Ireland champions and with only three minutes left they went in front again and although it was only by a point it looked as if they would hold out because many of the Galway players had left their best form, seemingly, behind them. Then a ball broke out to the right just into Kerry's half of the field as Galway attacked the Canal end goal, Mattie McDonagh, Galway's big and inspirational centre half-forward, ran for the ball. As two Kerrymen closed in on him Mattie stooped and grabbed the ball, turned and landed it over to the flying

Seamus Leydon, who careered towards the Kerry goal, side-stepped two defenders and though he seemed to be closing an impossible angle drove to the net. The final score: 1-7 to 0-8.

Ah, but did McDonagh lift the ball off the ground or raise it legitimately? The controversy raged for days. As the incident happened there were howls of protest from the Kerry spectators and some of the newspapers cast doubt on Mattie's 'lift' but from my position in the commentary box it was very, very difficult to say. It happened close enough to the sideline to mean that I was looking down on Mattie and couldn't really see if he had legally toed the ball into his hands. Galway, of course, were annoyed by the controversy, but as time went by they realised it wasn't about to affect their trip to America — something rare enough in those days to be still a very big prize. I was out in Gaelic Park for the two matches with New York, but didn't travel with the team as I was on duty on the Saturday at the Irish Sweeps Derby at the Curragh and only got to New York very late that night after a mad dash by small plane from the racecourse to Shannon and through Boston. But that's another story.

When I caught up eventually with the Galway party they related an amusing story. In the days after the home final we in the Sports Department of RTE attempted to resolve whether Mattie McDonagh had actually picked the ball off the ground or not. Now those were times long before the widespread availability of videotape, so even a National League final wasn't covered by the one and only outside broadcast unit then in the station's possession and we had to rely on 16 mm film — and black and white at that.

Nor could the station rise to the luxury of a slow-motion machine, but I encouraged our sports sub-editors to see what they and the people in the film editing section could do with the film of the incident. Eventually they managed to slow down the film frame by frame and we transmitted the results on the Thursday night *Sport In Action* programme. I must say that the film was so inconclusive that we invited viewers to make up their own minds. Some were convinced Mattie McDonagh had blatantly picked up the ball, others were sure he raised it properly with the toe. Now, Galway's representative on the Central Council of the GAA was Canon James O'Dea, the parish priest of Clarinbridge, and he had watched our replay of the incident on the Thursday night. At breakfast the following morning he asked his housekeeper if she had seen the programme and when she replied yes, she certainly had, he asked the relevant question: 'Well, did you think Mattie picked up the ball?' Remember television was still almost in its infancy in rural areas and the intricacies of it were little known to most viewers. So, according to the Galway players who told me this story, the good lady housekeeper in her innocence answered the Canon: 'You know, Canon, I really don't know, but whether he did or not wasn't Mattie a right fool to go out and do it again for the television!'

The National League final played in New York was the first to be decided over two legs with the aggregate score to count on the second Sunday (14 July), but ironically when this innovation was first proposed at Central Council it was vehemently opposed by Galway. Some months later their team was darned glad they hadn't got their way and that the aggregate system was introduced because they were beaten by a very good New York team 0-8 to 1-4 the first Sunday and it would have been a much bigger margin, I remember, but for two things: New York's terrible inaccuracy and the spectacular saves by Galway's goalkeeper Johnny Geraghty, whose display I raved about over the radio commentary back across the Atlantic. Galway certainly needed that second leg and Frank Stockwell, the only one of the three managers to make the trip, had them out in some very tough training sessions at Gaelic Park during the week. They took the whole thing so seriously that they declined the invitation from New York officials to make a day trip to Washington. Their determination really paid off in the second game as they won easily thanks to goals by Seamus Leydon, Christy Tyrrell and Mick Reynolds to take the title on the aggregate 4-12 to 0-17.

Because they were in New York so late into championship time Galway were granted the concession by the Connacht Council of a bye into the provincial final and they were hard pushed to overcome Sligo, who had a very fine team in those days, in that game. They had another close call from Down in the All-Ireland semi-final before qualifying for yet another meeting with Kerry. That wasn't a football game to be numbered among our cherished memories, but Galway, despite failing to score a goal again, retained the title — and to them that's what mattered most.

The following spring they lost their National League title when beaten by Longford in the home final and there was a dreadfully scary 60 minutes in the Connacht final when they just edged past Mayo with a winning point by Liam Sammon in injury time. The Galway players of that era were free in their tributes to the old rivals Mayo and I once heard John Donnellan say: 'In that sequence of years Mayo had a very good team and they ran us to close margins on a number of occasions and had it not been that Galway were that little bit better than them then Mayo might have been the team to win a few All-Irelands.'

Cork stood in Galway's way in the All-Ireland semi-final — one of the rare occasions in that period when they broke Kerry's Munster monopoly — and the final brought Meath into opposition, but long before the final whistle it was obvious that Galway's supreme confidence and team-work would enable them record the three-in-a-row. At last Galway scored a goal in an All-Ireland final: 1-10 to 0-7!

It was a marvellous achievement by Galway in the modern age. Remember it hadn't been done for a long time and I've already listed the teams that failed to do it in the quarter century since Kerry's completion of three-in-a-row in 1941. Moreover, since Galway's triumphs in the 1960s only Kerry again repeated it; that was in 1984–'86 as well, of course, as their four-in-a-row in 1978–'81. Even Kerry are included in the list of counties that have failed to take a third successive title in the last three decades: the Kingdom failing in 1971, Offaly 1973, Dublin 1978, Meath 1989 and Cork 1991.

But the end was approaching for the Galwaymen. They had gone through the league successfully and met Dublin in the home final on the last day of April 1967. They played with great determination, skill and lots of variety in their play to win 0-12 to 1-7. But that was the last victory. It sent them back to New York less than two weeks later and as I broadcast the first leg match against New York the physical and mental tiredness was very much in evidence. They were beaten 3-5 to 1-6 and lost again the following Sunday to go down 7-8 to 1-16 on the aggregate. But it must be said that New York had superb teams, skilful and very strong physically in those days, with players like Willie and Peter Nolan of Offaly, Peter Maguire (Kildare), Tommy Furlong (Offaly), Bren Tumulty (Wicklow) and Jimmy Foley (Kerry) who were still in their prime and the home team at Gaelic Park were worthy winners.

Galway were only a few weeks home when they were off again — this time to London and a meeting at Wembley Stadium with Cavan — and another defeat by a point. It was another warning signal. But they still went back into training fairly strenuously for the championship, which was now only two weeks away. I've often thought since then that because of the signs of tiredness now evident that it might have been much better if Galway had rested from football, and certainly from the physical exercises, in the fortnight before their clash with great rivals Mayo. They might have gone into that a lot fresher and the hard training could have been resumed later — if they'd overcome Mayo. But then that's hindsight talking. As it happened Galway's ambitions of four-in-a-row were shattered in their own Pearse Stadium on 25 June when they were routed by Mayo (3-13 to 1-8). So the reign ended in Salthill on that sunny day.

* * *

Another tremendous achievement in the 1960s was that of Tipperary. They won four championships and became known as the National League specialists with five triumphs in that competition. They had marvellous players from the unrelentingly tough full-back line of John Doyle, Michael Maher and Kieran Carey, to forwards like Liam Devaney, Donie Nealon, the impeccable and unerringly accurate Jimmy Doyle and the big bustling, but devastatingly effective, full-forward Sean McLoughlin. There was the outstanding Theo English in the middle of the field and, before the decade ended, the arrival of the elegant Mick Roche and superb forward Michael 'Babs' Keating. Great memories.

7

To Montrose via Laurel Park

Shortly after the Polo Grounds adventure in 1947 I was offered a nice 'perk' on the Hospitals Sweepstakes programme broadcast nightly on Radio Éireann. This was a soothing blend of dreamy, romantic music presented by the mellow-toned Bart Bastible which had been one of RÉ's principal sources of income almost since the foundation of the Sweeps Trust itself back in 1930.

Although it had an audience in Ireland estimated in the mid-1950s at around 750,000, it was in fact aimed primarily at listeners in Britain. Unable to advertise in English newspapers because it was against the law, the promoters of the Sweeps used radio as the best means of access to potential purchasers of tickets over there.

The spot I did on the show consisted of a well-informed bulletin on English racing which was sent to us from London, usually supplied by a racing journalist named Richard Baerlein. We always ended with 'my three best for tomorrow are...' I arrived into the studio in the GPO one evening to find that the 1,000-word script which normally awaited me was not there. I was due to fly to the United States the following day and, to tell the truth, was in no form to set about putting a piece together and select the tips but there was no way out. I duly named 'my three best' — they were all about 20/1 chances — and headed off to the US, not giving them another thought. When I next went to the studio I found a letter waiting for me telling me what a hero I was. It was from a man who said he had backed those 'well considered' tips and had been able to buy a pub from the proceeds!

About three years later I was in the Waldorf Hotel in London on a trip to the Epsom Derby and had ordered breakfast in my room. When the waiter arrived he deduced from the papers, race cards and field glasses that I was in town for the big race. As we chatted away he told me that there was a guy in Ireland who gave great tips and referred to the man, a friend of his, who had bought a pub on the basis of this master tipster's advice. Of course I got VIP treatment for the remainder of my stay when he discovered that I was this genius!

By this time my journalistic career at Independent Newspapers had moved on quite a bit. After some years on the subs' desk under sports editor Mitchel Cogley (Fred's father), I was promoted to racing correspondent succeeding a man called Tommy Carroll — in actual fact Tommy and I swopped jobs. Meanwhile the tempo of my life increased with every passing year and as surely as spring follows winter and summer spring, I would hop from Cheltenham to Croke Park, from Aintree to Fairyhouse, from Epsom to Semple Stadium to the Dublin Horse Show and then the ultimate excitement of the All-Ireland finals in September. Then, as the days grew shorter and autumn edged towards winter, I would take off on my annual sortie to America. This revolved around the Washington International, which had been devised to bridge the gap between the two quite different traditions of horse racing in the States and in Europe. Realising that the owners of crack thoroughbreds in France, England and Ireland would not risk their horses on American dirt tracks, John Schapiro, President of the plush Laurel Park Racecourse in Maryland, just outside Washington DC, had a turf track laid inside the existing cinders circuit and in 1952 staged the first Laurel International Race.

As I was very interested in the concept of international racing myself, I wrote to John Schapiro expressing a desire to see the next running of his race, and in due course I received an invitation to Laurel Park in November 1953. The fact that the Irish Derby winner, Chamier, owned by Mrs Frank Vickerman and trained by Vincent O'Brien had also been invited added spice to the trip. In the event the race had to be postponed for a week due to heavy snow which allowed plenty of time for sight-seeing. Each morning we went to the track and Charlie Smirke would take my wife Molly to the stables and point out 'the greatest certainty of all time'. The horse's name was Worden II, but no one believed him and it became a standing joke between us. When the race finally took place Charlie confounded the cynics and won in a canter on Worden II.

During the week's delay the jockeys, with time on their hands, hatched a plan to hire a plane to fly them to the bright lights of New York for a day. The part of the scheme that gave them the biggest kick was that John Schapiro should foot the bill for the plane. He was persuaded, on the strict understanding that this would be the first and last time that Laurel would be expected to supply this kind of service.

So began my long association with Laurel Park and John Schapiro. He and I became good friends and I was always happy to do my bit in promoting the race on our side of the Atlantic. John liked to do things in style and each year before the international he staged a magnificent reception for all the visitors and usually asked me to act as master of ceremonies. The guests always included the ambassadors to Washington of the countries represented in that year's race and I remember one particular *bon mot* by the Russian Ambassador when he was asked to speak on behalf of his country's team: 'On the turf, as well as under the turf, we are all equal', he told the distinguished gathering. How true. Another time when the Cold War was at its height a serious diplomatic incident threatened. It was in the days before starting stalls and that year the official starter, Eddie Blind, had difficulty getting the runners in line for the tape start. When he eventually let them away the Russian horse, Anagog, was left but ran on and despite the 20 lengths disadvantage managed to finish fourth. Nobody was unduly concerned until the phone rang in Schapiro's home at 2 a.m. the following morning. An irate Russian ambassador alleged that the authorities had deliberately selected a Hungarian lad to handle Anagog at the start with instructions to hold it back when the tape went up. The matter would be taken up at government level, John was informed.

His immediate reaction was to consult a neutral advisor: me. Having heard what the Ambassador had said I suggested he should wait to see what would happen in the cold light of the morning. Fortunately the affair had cooled off by then and no more was heard of it, although we wondered if a horse from the Soviet Union would ever appear at Laurel Park again. Lo and behold, the same Anagog returned the following year and finished third in an incident-free race.

My American racing connections paid off in other ways. I had seen how the meetings over there were greatly enhanced by a commentary which could be heard by the punters in the stands and resolved to introduce this innovation to Ireland. Jack Duggan, the manager at Gowran Park, agreed to try it out on an experimental basis and we arranged that the people attending the meeting would give their verdict on it. A coupon was printed on the race-card asking racegoers to vote on the idea. There were a few objectors who said they found the commentary distracting but by and large it was a huge success, an overwhelming 97% voting in favour. The course commentary soon became a feature of Irish racing and spread to British and European tracks too.

Another refinement which had a more important impact on the way racing is controlled was the Film Patrol: a record of every horse's running in every race. The information it provides is of enormous benefit to the Stewards when it comes to judging some of the more controversial aspects of racing, such as interference, horses running below form, jockeys' misdemeanours, etc. The Patrol idea came from Joe McGrath who had seen the system in operation in the US. He asked me to investigate further, so I made contact with a man named Marshall Cassidy — the 'Mr Racing of America' — to study their set-up and learn how to operate it. A special tower was constructed at the Curragh to house the camera, operated by Collie Farrell and pointing straight down the course so as to give a head-on view. When the film was developed the jockeys who had taken part in the race were asked into the Stewards' room to watch, and were amazed, not to say mortified, at the way it showed up all their various foibles and questionable tactics, in fact, every single detail.

It became one of my tasks to interpret the film for the Stewards. I remember one incident early on when a certain prominent steward called me to one side after viewing a particular race, saying he was perturbed that the film had not shown what he had seen happening in the race. Could he view it again, he wondered. Full of confidence in the 'honesty' of the Film Patrol, I was quite happy to accede to his request and, having watched it again, he too was convinced of its accuracy. His fellow stewards embraced this new tool enthusiastically and before long at the behest of the Turf Club it was installed at all Irish meetings.

The film records were a valuable resource for trainers, too, as they were entitled to ask for a viewing if they felt they needed to get a better picture of what had happened. I recall Francis Shortt thanking me once for having shown him how one particular race had gone. The Film Patrol became 'God' in any enquiry. Senior stewards from Britain and France came to see how it worked and soon it was in operation in their own countries. In the early days, the Film Patrol used actual celluloid stock but the video era came about somewhat fortuitously. One day on the way to the Curragh, the Film Patrol truck was involved in an accident, turned over in a ditch and was out of commission. As an emergency measure video was tried with immediate success and was used instead of film thereafter.

Throughout the late 1940s and the 1950s, that is in the years before Telefis Éireann came into being, there were others like myself who did sports commentaries for Radio Éireann on a freelance basis. The late Eamonn Andrews tried his hand at several sports, including soccer, but he proved to be outstanding at the ringside and eventually took over from the Canadian Stuart McPherson and Raymond Glendenning as the BBC's voice of boxing and presenter of their Saturday afternoon flagship programme, *Sports Report*. Dr Ronnie Thornton commentated on rugby as did another man who was to become a well-known doctor, Austin Darragh, and later on Ireland's fortunes on the rugby field were described by Joe Linanne, Bill Twomey from Cork, and Liam Browne who doubled as an athletics expert. Brian Durnin, who was in the Department of External Affairs and who rose to the rank of ambassador, had a go at soccer commentaries before Philip Greene and Kieran Kenealy took over the big occasions at Dalymount Park and elsewhere. Barry Mason was one of the team involved in the innovative and surprisingly extensive coverage given to motor racing in those early days.

The GAA folk had been served on a regular basis for many years by the Sunday night results programme which Seán Ó Ceallacháin organised single-handedly until he was eventually succeeded by his son, Seán Óg, happily still going strong. Now more than fifty years in existence, *GAA Sports Results*, still has dedicated listeners all over this country and Britain, and nowadays, thanks to satellite broadcasting, in many other corners of the world. Also broadcast on Sunday throughout the 1950s was *Soccer Survey*. Tony Sheehan took this on when the original presenter, J. L. Brennan, a prominent soccer official, died.

One sports programme I have not mentioned up to now was *Sports Stadium*. This started around 1950 and was organised originally by Gus Ingoldsby and presented by Eamonn Andrews. It went out on Friday evenings and was largely concerned with discussions with various sports journalists and previews about forthcoming events but it was not a magazine programme like the ones I had heard on American radio. So, when the opportunity presented itself to launch a Monday morning sponsored programme about sport I jumped at it. The *Vaseline Hair Tonic Programme*, as it was called, was a chance for me to offer listeners interested in sport something different. Putting it together was quite a business. Each Sunday evening I would go to the Harcourt Street studios of Arks Advertising Agency and deliver myself into the hands of a brilliant and ingenious producer/technician named Bill Stapleton.

I would arrive with a head full of ideas, a few headlines scribbled on the back of an envelope, a record from a series *Great Fights of the Century* that I had picked up overseas and maybe an interview I had done at the week-end on a new-fangled tape recorder. I never knew how Bill made it all work so well but he never failed and, come what may, got the transmission recording to the Radio Éireann supervisor in Henry Street on schedule.

The Vaseline programme ran for 12 years and I must say I regretted having to give it up when my situation in broadcasting changed in 1961. It was good fun while it lasted and provided me with valuable programme-making experience for the challenges that lay ahead. Looking back I have mostly fond memories of Bill Stapleton and his very willing and cheerful assistants, Willie and Kieran.

In August 1960 I was contacted at the *Irish Independent* by Paul Warren of the Telefis Éireann Authority, inviting me to sit on an interview panel for the selection of the Head of Sport for the embryonic television station. Twelve people were to be interviewed, he told me. At a break in the proceedings Eamonn Andrews, then a member of the TÉA and chairman of the interview board, asked me why I was on the interviewing side and not a candidate myself. Until then I had viewed my role in broadcasting purely as a part-timer and felt I needed to stay with the 'day job' because I could not survive on the morsels I was picking up at the microphone. The subject was not carried any further at that stage and the interviews continued. When we talked again at lunch Andrews was even keener on the idea of my taking the job. By the end of that week I had received an offer at terms which I could not refuse and I did not. This job was mine from September 1960 until I left for Leopardstown Racecourse in 1972.

My first task in this new role was to establish contact with the various sporting organisations around the country and negotiate television coverage of all the major events as cheaply as possible. These discussions met with varying degrees of success. The GAA agreed that we could cover their matches for a nominal fee of £10 per match! The fact that Paddy O'Keeffe, the far-seeing general secretary of that organisation, was on the TÉA certainly facilitated this arrangement. Racing and boxing also featured prominently in Telefís sports coverage in the early days. Soccer posed some problems and it was my impression that its official body were basing their demands on what was happening in television in Britain rather than on the situation of the fledgling service Telefís Éireann then was. Rugby was another difficulty as the IRFU already had an arrangement in place with the BBC for Ireland's matches in the Five Nations Championship. Happily all these obstacles were overcome in time.

Meanwhile there were programmes to be made. The resources to make them in those breathlessly exciting early days were very limited but the enthusiasm of those around me was boundless, particularly on the staff side. At my right hand was my secretary, Oonagh Gormley, and at my left, Esther Byrne, the Sports Department's production assistant. Both had good sporting pedigrees. Oonagh was a daughter of George Gormley, the Sports Editor of the *Evening Mail*. Before joining Telefís Éireann she had worked as secretary to that great Dublin character and renowned athletics promoter-cum-optician, Billy Morton. Esther's father and brother, Mick Byrne senior and junior, were both very well known racing journalists and good friends of mine. (Her sister, Frankie, would later become a celebrity in her own right as 'Dear Frankie' offering sharp and witty advice to the lovelorn on the Jacobs–sponsored radio programme.) Philip Greene was another original member of the Sports Department. He had been Sports Officer under the old Radio Éireann regime and, while I concentrated my attentions almost exclusively on the TV side, he continued to look after sport on the senior service. Within a couple of months of setting up shop in Montrose we were joined by two former colleagues of mine in Independent House, Fred Cogley and Maurice Quinn. On the performing side in TV Sport, our front man was Brendan O'Reilly, the handsome Irish high jump record holder then just recently returned from the States. Phil Thompson, an Englishman with little or no experience of sport or indeed of things Irish, was the first producer assigned to the department, and like the rest of us he had to learn fast. Within a year he had moved on to other things and was replaced by a wise-cracking American named Burt Budin who had the priceless capacity of remaining cool no matter what the crisis and there were many of those, I can tell you.

The Department's first major venture was an outside broadcast from Leopardstown. It was not, to put it mildly, the most perfect broadcast ever transmitted but we put it down to experience. There was simply no time to dwell on our mistakes.

I have much more vivid memories of the very first outside broadcast by TÉ which was, of course, the opening night, 31 December, 1960. One of my roles was to interview the occupants of the Top Table in the ballroom of the Gresham Hotel. These were to be the key members of the Authority. Imagine my surprise and that of the floor manager who was to cue me (he was Peter Collinson who went on to make a name for himself as a film director) when minutes before we were due to begin we saw on the monitors that Ed Roth, the Director General, and the other people we were to interview, were still, large as life, in Montrose. There was no escape so we went on air and, making the best of the situation, interviewed anyone we could recognise. Austin Clarke, the poet, and Frank Glennon, a well-known soccer and racing personality, were among the victims. At least one of those I did aim my microphone at had been celebrating for quite some time and was not a suitable candidate for interview! Somehow though we kept going and filled in the time until the VIPs arrived from Montrose before retiring outside where the high-spirited crowd that had gathered in O'Connell Street were pasting Patrick O'Hagan, the singer, with snowballs.

One incident in the early days which caused a few very anxious hours in Montrose was when Fred Cogley went to Paris to cover a rugby international. All the necessary arrangements had been made, lines had been booked and no problems were anticipated. When the time came to call in Fred in Paris we were greeted with silence. The

BBC commentary was substituted while frantic efforts were made to contact our man. Time passed, the match was over and still there was no word from Fred. Our worries lasted until 7 p.m. that evening when Fred phoned to check how the broadcast had gone. He had commentated on the whole match as planned and was mystified as to why we had heard none of it. It turned out that TV viewers in an obscure French colony somewhere in Africa had benefitted from Fred's spiel because he had been shown to the wrong commentary position by the organisers of the TV coverage. All was well, Fred was safe and we at least had had a commentary we could understand.

Paris was the scene of another more amusing incident I remember. I was at Longchamp covering the Prix de l'Arc de Triomphe and Michael O'Carroll was producing in Montrose. Before the race the French TV people were testing the feeds to all the various countries taking the race by transmitting the output of some of their cameras. One of the French cameramen with a Gallic sense of fun spotted the glamorous Elizabeth Taylor in the parade ring and focused long and lovingly on every inch of her voluptuous figure. To my consternation during these shots Michael cued me that we were on air and I found myself groping for suitable phrases to describe this glamorous close-up. I got the word about four minutes later from the French crew member on the spot that we were in fact due on air a few seconds later and so my well chosen (!) words had not actually been broadcast to the Irish nation.

One sport which got good coverage in the early years of Telefís Éireann was boxing. Well-known referee Charlie Higgins was the chief organiser of a competition we ran in conjunction with the IABA for novice and unknown boxers and a ring, with all the trappings, was installed in Studio One for these programmes. One evening there was a bit of a panic when one of the competitors failed to turn up but Charlie, who was to referee the bout, was not a bit put out. He persuaded a young man from the audience, who was about the right weight but who had little or no experience, to don the gloves. It was like watching an artist at work to see the way Charlie manoeuvred the two men round the ring so as to protect the novice. The climax of the series was a gala night at which Joe Louis, no less, presented the prizes to the winners.

One of our coups in the early 1960s was the broadcast of a world heavyweight title fight between Floyd Patterson and Sonny Liston. Ed Roth, the first Director General, was very keen on the idea and gave us the go-ahead. A good friend of mine, Barney Nagle, a boxing journalist in the States, helped to set it up, and we dispatched Noel Andrews to Chicago with instructions to get a position as close to the ring as possible so as to be able to get a few post-fight words with the winner if it could be managed at all. When the fight ended Noel moved like lightning and beat the other commentators to the punch, so to speak. The only one who got there before him was Cassius Clay who also wanted to be among the first to congratulate Liston. So, making the most of the situation, Noel interviewed them both. Imagine his chagrin when he got back to his position and discovered that the sound engineer had turned off his interview microphone, so Irish television viewers missed out on what should have been their first taste of the future Mohammed Ali.

In June 1963 all the resources of the 18-month-old Irish television service were concentrated on its first major challenge of international importance, the State visit of John F. Kennedy. I was asked by the new Director General, Gunnar Rugheimer, to commentate on the main events of the visit and in the weeks leading up to it I was involved in helping to pick camera positions in the streets of Dublin. On one such mission I got out of my car near Nelson's Pillar, telling the Garda on duty what we were at and asking if I could park my car there. He was very co-operative but made a crack about me not really deserving any help because of what I had done to his father. It seemed his father had invested in some of my tips which, I gathered, were not my best. Nevertheless, he allowed Burt Budin and the rest of the crew to get on with their work. On the morning JFK arrived I was installed in Montrose in front of monitors showing pictures from all the different cameras. For some unexplained reason President de Valera, who was due to greet Kennedy at the airport, was still at Áras an Úachtarán as the visitor's plane was seen approaching Dublin Airport. There followed a mad dash as he was whisked from the Park via the back roads to Collinstown. Meanwhile Air Traffic Control delayed Air Force 1 until our President appeared, fully composed, on the tarmac.

The day passed without further hitches from our point of view and when President Kennedy went to bed that night we headed for

Dunganstown, his ancestral home which he was due to visit the next day. When we rose early to see how things had been arranged we were told that the President would be at one end of a room and we were warned by the bodyguards that there were to be no TV microphones placed anywhere near him. Unimpressed by these security arrangements, one of our crew, a floor manager from Harlech Television, suggested, with a twinkle in his eye, that I take a walk while, without my say-so or anyone else's, he descended from the TV scaffolding tower, dived under the tables and set up a microphone near the forbidden area. He then crept back and took up his position again. We settled down to await JFK's arrival and, sure enough, when he reached his end of the room he jokingly picked up the microphone and tested it, thus letting it be seen that he realised it was there. It stayed there and picked up quite an amount of the President's conversation, thus undoubtedly improving the coverage. By the time it came for the Kennedy party to leave from Shannon I was at the Curragh, covering the Irish Derby, and my next assignment involving JFK was in much sadder circumstances.

Molly and I had travelled over to Laurel as usual in November of 1963. The evening before our departure for home we were packing our bags in the hotel when Molly called me to come and look at the TV. All programmes had just been interrupted with the rumour that the President had been shot. Five minutes later the story was confirmed and, of course, the television stations stayed with it as the terrible details unfolded. I picked up the phone to contact the newsroom in Telefís Éireann and explained where I was. They promised to ring back and in shocked and tearful silence Molly and I sat glued to the television. A short time later Pearse Kelly, the Head of News, got through and asked me to arrange television coverage of the funeral with NBC. The American stations, it turned out, got together to organise combined coverage of the funeral and were making it available to other countries, so this posed no problem. Kelly went on to say that Telefís wanted me to stay over and do the commentary.

It was down to work then as I set about briefing myself as thoroughly as was humanly possible about the funeral arrangements and particularly about the very many foreign dignitaries who were expected and whom I would have to be able to identify. We hired a second TV to help us collect information, and familiarise ourselves with names and faces. We heard that General McKeown, the Army Chief-of-Staff, and a group of cadets were coming from Ireland so I went out to the airport to meet them. President de Valera and Frank Aiken, the Minister for External Affairs, were on the same plane. After a few words with General McKeown, who said he and his men had not yet been told what role they would play in the ceremonies I headed back to the hotel through streets full of people weeping and wandering around in a dazed state.

For the funeral itself we were allocated a commentary position at the NBC studios, gazing at three monitors. There was just Molly, myself and an engineer working for Telefis. Our position was next to the BBC for whom Richard Dimbleby was on duty. He recognised me as the 'man from the Grand National' and very graciously offered us any help his team of researchers and assistants could give us. 'We're all in the same boat' was how he put it.

Before we went on the air I spoke to Tom Hardiman, the man in charge at the Dublin end and requested that no one contact me over the headphones during the coverage. I felt strongly that any interruption to my concentration would disturb the flow and mood of the commentary. This request was respected and there followed four hours of silence from Dublin. But, of course, I wondered whether we were getting through at all so at one stage I asked Molly to phone Dublin to find out. The answer was in the affirmative.

All the homework we had done paid dividends and I was able to add colour to the black and white pictures by, for example, describing the scenes inside St Malachy's Cathedral from my memories of having been at Mass there the previous day. It was a gruelling session both emotionally and physically and I was exhausted when it was over. The following day, as life in New York returned to normal, Molly and I went to the pictures to relax and unwind a bit. The movie we saw was *It's A Mad, Mad, Mad World*. So it was.

8

Broadcasting Here, There and Everywhere

It's fair to say that most people knew me, or nowadays remember me, as a broadcaster, but it shouldn't be overlooked that I worked for many years as a newspaper journalist, too, and enjoyed that side of my life immensely. I joined the sport staff of the *Irish Independent* in 1944. Not long afterwards I became their chief Irish racing correspondent, a position that took me to the more famous racetracks around the world. At the time I was broadcasting for Radio Éireann on a freelance basis and did so until 1961 when I was appointed Head of Sport to the newly-established Radio Telefís Éireann prior to the start-up of the new television service. But at the beginning of my working life, and ever afterwards, broadcasting was my first love and it has taken me around the globe and into some very diverse situations — some wonderful, some even weird. To this day I regard the commentary on the 1947 All-Ireland football final played at the Polo Grounds in New York as the most exciting and most memorable of all my broadcasts, certainly on hurling or football, but very much on a par with it has to be my 'Foinavon Grand National' at Aintree in 1967.

Imagine my deep disappointment then when the next opportunity arose to return to New York and broadcast again from the Polo Grounds but I was denied the chance. That was September 1951. The previous year the New York hurling and football teams had been admitted to the National League finals by the Central Council of the GAA and their football team had created a huge sensation by beating Cavan at Croke Park in July 1950. Needless to say there was, therefore, very great interest in the 1951 finals which were to be played at the Polo Grounds between New York and the home winners, Meath in football and Galway in hurling. Of course, I was all set to go across the Atlantic again especially after having got great praise for the 1947 broadcast. Moreover, Radio Éireann had agreed that I should travel and they had hoped that the same arrangements that had obtained for the 1947 final would be worked out again with the GAA — i.e. the station paying for the broadcast circuits from America and the GAA covering the travel and accommodation costs for a commentator. In fact Radio Éireann had already booked the broadcast lines at a cost of £300, a not inconsiderable sum in those days. However, the association demurred when it came to repeating the financial arrangements in 1951 believing that it was an expense they couldn't undertake for National League finals. So the president at the time, Mícheál Kehoe from Wexford, was given the task of securing the services of a commentator in New York when he travelled out some weeks before to make arrangements with the New York officials for the finals.

Paddy O'Keeffe, the general secretary of the association, broke the news to me that the commentator would be someone called Lefty Devine. For all I knew he might have been the greatest commentator in the world, another Bill Stern, who was then regarded as America's best. I was utterly shocked and was in no way mollified when told that this move would save the GAA the cost of my trip. I tried to get Paddy 'O' to have the decision changed but on my next visit to him in his Croke Park office I was told there was nothing he could do as the council were anxious to save the expense of sending a commentator from Ireland. So who was Lefty Devine? American-born John Lawrence Devine was a sportswriter with the *Irish World* weekly newspaper in New York and he had been 'announcing' the matches at Gaelic Park since about 1945. He was, therefore, very familiar with the New York players, not so with the visiting Meath and Galway teams and had never done a full non-stop radio commentary. Even though I say so myself, it was a recipe for disaster.

I left Paddy O'Keeffe's office in a rage and told him I would never broadcast again ... and I meant it! Then the news broke that I wouldn't be travelling and on the morning of the All-Ireland football final (23 September) the *Sunday Independent* printed the story under the headline 'You'll Hear Him To-day But Not Next Sunday' and went on to state that the 'GAA authorities at home — at least a majority of them —have refused to incur the expense of bringing O'Hehir to New

York.' It added that I would be broadcasting the Mayo-Meath final that day in Croke Park, but not from New York the following Sunday.

When it came to the broadcast that Sunday night (30 September) the commentary was only about five minutes old when I was dancing around the room with glee. Lefty tried his best, introduced many Americanisms, as it were, and christened the Meath full-back Paddy 'Hands' O'Brien, but proved that he was no radio commentator and the whole broadcast was a Grade A flop. This was the general opinion backed up by the newspapers the next day and one of them stated 'that O'Hehir was divine to forgive Devine.' Even one sportswriter who in the next-day's *Irish Press* wrote somewhat favourably of Lefty's commentary had to admit in his Tuesday column that he had been inundated with phone calls from angry readers disagreeing with his views and deploring the broadcast. The GAA even admitted that it had made a mistake and Paddy O'Keeffe, who was one of my greatest supporters from my first broadcast and a firm friend, told me that the point had been made and asked me to reconsider my position about future commentaries. It didn't take me long to make up my mind on that and, in fairness, I must say that Lefty Devine became a good friend on my many subsequent trips to New York and Gaelic Park. When the next teams travelled out to America — Mayo footballers and Cork hurlers in 1954 for new competitions called the St Brendan Cups — I was the commentator in the Polo Grounds. And there were many more broadcasts from there and from Gaelic Park in the following years.

I also worked for many broadcasting organisations apart from RTE including the BBC and the three American networks — ABC, CBS and NBC — at one time or another. In 1959 I got the BBC interested in hurling and encouraged them to come over for the All-Ireland final that year. The opening of the then new Hogan Stand allowed filming because, for the first time, Croke Park now had a proper camera area and from this box a BBC cameraman filmed the Waterford-Kilkenny drawn game on the first Sunday of September. Kenneth Wolstenholme, who was their main soccer commentator at the time, came over with the crew and the feature built around the final was broadcast on their midweek *Sportsview* programme. The cameraman was an Indian, who had played hockey at a very high level in both India and England, and he and Wolstenholme were so impressed with the hurling that they travelled back to Croke Park for the replay a month later at their own expense since the BBC weren't covering the second game. That replay marked the first senior appearance on the Kilkenny team for Eddie Keher, who had played in the minor curtain-raiser the previous month.

Another exciting venture to be involved in during the 1950s was the relay of the All-Ireland finals to the African continent. In that period Radio Éireann had no full-time sports people on the staff and organisation of the sports broadcasts was looked after by Gus Ingoldsby whose title was staff administration officer.

Over the years Ingoldsby found that there was great interest among the Irish missionaries in sporting events at home and they continuously bombarded Radio Éireann with letters asking if there was any way the commentaries could be relayed to Africa, as their only contact, and that of exiles all over America too, with the games was through newspapers which took weeks to reach their destinations. A survey was carried out and it was found that most of the demand for the broadcasts came from all over the African continent so the help of the Department of External Affairs was sought in finding a station that would be willing to co-operate in the venture. Two very powerful transmitters broadcast over Africa at the time for shortwave stations — Radio Brazzaville in French Equatorial Africa and Radio Leopoldville in the Belgian Congo. Brazzaville it seemed had the stronger signal of the two and their help was sought through the Department, whose secretary then was one Conor Cruise O'Brien. After some negotiation Radio Brazzaville agreed to relay the commentary of the 1953 Kerry-Armagh football final on their network.

The response to Radio Éireann was overwhelming and hundreds of letters and cablegrams poured into the station over the next few days, some of them from as far away as Queensland in Australia, Italy and Sweden as well as from all parts of Africa. The shortwave transmission was even heard on a ship in Hong Kong harbour and there was a report from Chicago that the reception was very clear.

All of this suggested that there was a great need for an Irish shortwave station, an idea that had already been mooted in the late 1940s. Radio Éireann had even purchased the transmitters and test transmissions were about to be carried out in April 1948, but by then there had been a change of government and in May that year the new Minister for Finance, Paddy McGilligan, announced that the shortwave project would be abandoned, along with, it might be added, the proposed trans-Atlantic air service. Although the flights to America were eventually inaugurated in 1958, the shortwave station was never resurrected. Nowadays, of course, shortwave broadcasts have been superseded by satellite and other means of transmission.

Still the reaction to those Radio Brazzaville broadcasts was so enthusiastic that Radiodiffusion et Télévision Francaises (RTF) in France, which controlled Radio Brazzaville, asked Radio Éireann to supply further programmes and one of those provided was 'Balladmakers Christmas.' The broadcasts of the All-Ireland finals through Brazzaville, as well as some Railway Cup finals on St Patrick's Day, continued into the early 1960s with most of them recorded by RÉ and transmitted to Paris for broadcast on the day after the finals — an arrangement eventually found to be most suitable because of heavy use of the broadcast circuits at Paris on Sundays. The last finals to be broadcast on Radio Brazzaville were the 1961 All-Ireland finals (Tipperary-Dublin and Down-Offaly).

It was a great pity they had to stop because they provided a very welcome service to the many Irish people spread all over the world. Although there are not now as many missionaries in foreign parts, especially Africa, as there were, this is probably made up for by the number of lay voluntary aid workers from Ireland who would surely be delighted to hear the finals broadcast. But for one reason or another—mainly the home station diverting most of its resources and energies into the planned new television service which went on the air on New Year's Eve 1961 — the broadcasts through Radio Brazzaville were discontinued after 1961. Even more ironically, RTE made arrangements to have the 1996 All-Ireland finals broadcast overseas — again on shortwave — with the help of a German station.

Through my connection with the Laurel Park racetrack and its owner, John Schapiro, I made contacts with the American networks. On one occasion my commentary at the course was carried on the CBS radio network and another time I approached ABC, long before Telefis Éireann came into existence, with the idea of their covering the All-Ireland finals, the Irish Derby and possibly the Horse Show. It was on one visit to the ABC headquarters on West 66th Street in New York that I first met Roone Arledge, who was their president in charge of sport, and Barney Nagle, one of their sports producers. A few years later I was involved with ABC in their coverage of the Laurel Park race working with Arledge, producer Chris Schenkel and the ex-jockey Eddie Arcaro who was a wonderful character.

Arledge had revolutionized sports coverage on American television and in addition to making live coverage more and more dramatic he played a very big part in building up ABC's Saturday afternoon magazine programme *Wide World of Sports* which, as the name implies. included sports from all over the world. He was so successful as the boss of the sports department that in 1977 he was also made president of the news division and for a time he filled both positions before leaving sport to somebody else.

Their *Wide World of Sports* was hugely popular and it made its presenter a household name in the US. He was the Irish-American journalist from Baltimore, Jim McManus, known professionally as Jim McKay. He was ABC's main presenter and became even more famous for a marvellous marathon feat of broadcasting from the 1972 Munich Olympics when 11 members of the Israeli team were murdered by Black September Arab terrorists. ABC was the 'Olympic network' at that time and they stayed on the air live from Munich on that dreadful day (5 September); McKay was the chief anchorman for their output and he was on the air continuously for 16 hours presenting coverage of the events from both sports and news journalists.

Arledge and McKay were a superb combination and eventually I persuaded them to come to Ireland having interested them in hurling. Their first visit was in September 1964 for the Tipperary-Kilkenny All-Ireland final which was shown on *Wide World of Sports* the following Saturday. The procedure was that they took away the tape of RTE's full coverage of the match with my commentary but Jim McKay and myself would tape special additional introductory and explanatory interviews for the American viewers. Having checked my measurements, the Americans arrived over with a special ABC Sports blazer for me to wear during those interviews.

Those weren't their only visits. They broadcast the 1965 Irish Sweeps Derby at the Curragh and their coverage of that race was the first European horse race to be transmitted live to the US. Because of its importance Roone Arledge himself travelled with the production team for an event that was being relayed across the Atlantic on the Early Bird satellite. My involvement that day led to one of the most exciting, if hectic, weekends I ever had because in addition to being RTE's television commentator on the big race I was also due in Gaelic Park, New York, the following day to commentate for RTE radio on the first leg of the Galway versus New York National Football League final.

Additionally some of the ABC people, including Arledge, McKay and a producer, Chuck Howard, were anxious to be back in the US by the Sunday also. But how were we to get to New York by the next day with the Aer Lingus New York flight due to depart long before we would be finished with the Derby coverage? Enter Bart Cronin of the airline's press and public relations office. Having put the problem to him and emphasised the importance of the visiting television people in relation to the goodwill they could create for Ireland, Bart took the matter to his superiors and they came up with the solution that their Boston flight, due to leave later than the one for New York, would take-off from Dublin but would be held in Shannon to await our arrival from the Curragh. Arrangements were made for me and the ABC personnel to be picked up from the centre of the Curragh and rushed to Shannon on three small planes hired especially for the occasion.

That Derby was won by Meadow Court, which was owned by American millionaire Max Bell. A few days previously he had sold a one-third share of the horse to the crooner Bing Crosby. Bing made the journey to Ireland especially for the race and after the horse gave Lester Piggott his first Irish classic win I believe Bing sang a few ditties in celebration. But myself and the ABC people were not around to hear him. As soon as the race ended I handed the microphone over to Tony Power of the *Irish Press* who was to commentate on the next race, the 3.30, and along with the Americans I scampered down the grandstand and across the racecourse before we all piled into the small planes which were already revving up for the flight to Shannon.

By now, however, the weather had turned foul and it lashed rain as we made our way south-west. I was in the first plane with McKay and Arledge and we got to Shannon without incident, but Chuck Howard was in a small aircraft which had a leak in one of the windows and this was noticed only on the way down from the Curragh. The result was that Chuck arrived at Shannon absolutely drenched and, of course, with no chance to change clothes; for two reasons: remember the Aer

Lingus plane was already late waiting on the tarmac for us and our luggage had already been checked into the baggage compartment.

I don't know what explanation had been given to the passengers for the delay of this Boston flight, but I do remember that we all got a very frosty reception when we boarded the plane as the other travellers did not appreciate being held up for television people. Eventually we got to Boston and I had to dash again to change from one terminal to another at Logan airport to catch a domestic flight to New York where I arrived later that night after a long, long day. However, a good night's sleep and I was in Gaelic Park ready for the football match the next day. When I caught up with the Galway players and officials, Father Paddy Mahon and Frank Stockwell, they told me that they had been watching us on the ABC broadcast in their Manhattan hotel rooms the previous morning.

ABC Television also came to Croke Park for a Railway Cup hurling final between Leinster and Munster in the mid-1970s and at this time they had a 'colour' man with them on the team along with Jim McKay. As was the custom with American networks then, and still is, he was a famous sportsman himself and after the game they asked me to take them to the winning Leinster dressing-room. This superstar wanted to meet some of the players as he was so impressed with the skill and speed of the game — and the fact that the players wore no padding! Eddie Keher, who was a main contributor to Leinster's victory that day, recalls: 'In comes this tall, black American who was with the visiting television people. We were told he was the "Christy Ring of American football". I'll never forget his name: O.J. Simpson!' Soon after that ABC lost interest in Irish sport, but another American network, NBC, introduced a programme called *SportsWorld* and came over for the All-Ireland hurling finals on a few occasions.

At that time I was very much involved with NBC — along with Brough Scott of ITV — in their coverage of the Breeder's Cup series of races which began in the early 1980s. Brough and myself were used as both interviewees, assessing foreign entries, and interviewers of some of the personalities at the races. NBC took the RTE coverage of the hurling finals, like ABC before them, and dressed it up into an edited package for later transmission, usually shown around the St Patrick's Day weekend. But their interest came to an end with the more widespread distribution of the live close-circuit television showing of the All-Ireland finals throughout various centres in the major cities across the States.

One of the highlights of my broadcasting career was to take part in the great adventure of Meath's tour of Australia in March 1968. It was truly an adventure — a pioneering endeavour that opened up new avenues which eventually led to Kerry touring 'Down Under'. But more importantly it was an indirect precursor of the trips by Irish teams for the compromise rules internationals in 1986 and 1990. An interest in matches between Gaelic football teams and sides from the Australian code was first expressed in the mid-1960s during the presidency of Alf Murray when the then Victorian League champions, Geelong, contacted Alf about the possibility of their side touring Ireland. Murray was particularly enthusiastic, but nothing came of the proposal mainly because Geelong went into something of a decline after winning the 'premiership' in 1967.

It was then left to one Harry Beitzel to give the whole thing a kick start, as it were. Harry was a prominent umpire (or referee as we would know him) in the Rules game, but he was also a prominent salesman and public relations person with a leading petroleum company and, as we all came to realise as we got to know him better, someone who was very impatient with the somewhat staid and, it seemed, immovable administrators of Australian Football. So along with one of that game's greatest stars now a prominent coach, Ron Barassi, Harry got together a team of leading players from the Victorian League for a 'world' tour taking in Dublin, London and New York.

Beitzel had sent word ahead to the GAA that the Aussie team wished to play the best in Ireland, meaning an international team. But since those were times prior to the selection even of the All-Stars the best in the GAA's view was the All-Ireland champions. However, only on the arrival of the Australian party in Dublin was this made clear to the champions — so Meath had just two days to get a team together for the game at Croke Park, which on 29 October was just five weeks after their All-Ireland victory and the countywide celebrations that had followed it. Not the best way to prepare for a meeting with footballers, even then semi-professionals, who proved to be super athletes. It was a very humbling experience for the All-Ireland champions who were hammered 3-16 to 1-10. But made worse by the fact that Peter

McDermott, their coach, gave his team a piece of dressing-room advice, which he freely admitted afterwards, caused him many red-faced blushes. Before they trotted out onto the field the Meath players were reminded by Peter that the Australians were playing Gaelic football for the first time, so if Meath got an early lead they weren't to rub it in. In fact, he ordered them 'to take it easy'. The Australians then went to London where they staged an exhibition which they firmly believed would be attended by a horde of expatriate Australians, but which turned out to be a financial disaster as only a little over 1,000 people turned up in contrast to the 23,419 at Croke Park. So Beitzel was quickly on the phone to Seán Ó Siocháin then the general secretary of the GAA, and they hastily arranged another match for the following Saturday when Mayo, the Connacht champions, provided the opposition before 20,121.

Immediately after that game the Aussies departed for Dublin airport and travelled to New York on a flight specially arranged for them by Aer Lingus so that they could play New York in Gaelic Park the following day. They left behind them an invitation to Meath to travel to Australia the following spring and those in charge of Meath, Peter McDermott and their trainer, Father Paddy Tully who was also chairman of the Meath County Board, were determined that the invitation would be accepted. But first a huge project of fund raising had to be undertaken after the County Board and then the Central Council gave their approval. The fund-raising campaign was highly successful and when the audited accounts were drawn up after the team's return to Ireland it was seen that there was a surplus of £18 on a tour that cost £20,082, a quarter of which was covered by a guarantee from the Australians and £1,000 contributed by the Central Council of the GAA.

It was a remarkable tour and one I will never forget. There was personal enjoyment in it for me apart from the actual success of the organisational and competitive aspects of it. Molly came with me because it afforded an opportunity to visit her brothers Dick and Paddy who now lived in Perth. So we travelled ahead of Meath and were there in Perth to meet them when they arrived on 6 March. Thus began one of the most successful tours ever undertaken by any GAA party. Many people contributed significantly to it, but two in particular: here in Ireland Peter McDermott, who worked with almost obsessive zeal to get the team to Australia, and at the other end, Harry Beitzel, a marvellous and meticulous organiser.

The most memorable feature of this trip was the utter determination of everyone in the Meath party to represent their county, their country and Gaelic football in the best way possible. Their earnestness was made all the stronger by the memory of the hammering they had taken from the Aussies five months earlier. This was noticeable in their attention to severe training on bitterly cold winter nights in January and February — a time of year during which such training was unheard of even in the latter half of the 1960s. The Meath officials had floodlighting lamps installed at Pairc Tailteann in Navan and the players trained under their glow on ground that was often solidly frozen.

It was a very different kind of hard pitch the team encountered when they arrived in Oz. Remember down there they were just emerging from their long summer and the weather was still very warm. Among the many people who helped Meath prepare for these conditions was Dr Felix McKnight, the former Armagh full-back, who was living in Perth with his wife, the former Delia McCartan of the famed Down football clan. In that city we visited Archbishop Raymond 'Mundy' Prenderville, who had won an All-Ireland medal with Kerry in 1924 and been expelled from All Hallows Seminary, which was across the road from the home I grew up in. He had slipped out to Croke Park for the final even though refused permission by the authorities. It obviously didn't do his career in the Church any harm as he was installed archbishop at the early age of 31.

Generally the football played on this tour was Gaelic football with some concessions allowed to the Australians like the direct pick-up. This was the way the Australians wanted it when they came to Dublin and they were confident (arrogant?) enough to suggest that they could successfully challenge the Irish at our game. They were right in that assumption as far as the games in Ireland were concerned. But what a very different story in Australia when Meath toured. Admittedly it was Meath's own sport, but they were under severe disadvantages. Not the least of them was playing fives matches in just nine days, something no GAA team had ever previously experienced. And those games were played in conditions to which they were totally unaccustomed, even in our hottest summer: they began in Perth where it was 93° F on 9

March and it was 97° for the last game in Melbourne on 17 March. I had done television highlights coverage of some of the games, but for the deciding 'test' at the Carlton club ground on St Patrick's Day I did live radio commentary which was heard back in Ireland at 9 o'clock in the morning. It was already turning out to be a miserably wet national holiday, as I discovered later on our return, so my comments on the severe heat and humidity in Melbourne during that broadcast must have aggravated my listeners. The ball was thrown in at that match by George Colley, then the Minister for Industry and Commerce who was on a trade mission to Melbourne at the time.

As the Meath players trained in Perth for the first game grave doubts were expressed about their fitness, notably by a leading newspaper columnist and some Aussie football officials. The visiting players were referred to, uncharitably and sarcastically, as 'midgets' because not many of them were over, or even touching, six feet compared with the Australian players who were all six feet and more, with Len Thompson standing at 6 ft 7 ins. But before they left Melbourne the All-Ireland champions were being called the 'mighty Meath midgets' by the sports writers. Especially after running the pride of the Victorian League, the strongest in all Australia and the division with the best players, 'off their feet' as it were, first on 11 March, a public holiday, before 28,000 at the famous Melbourne Cricket Ground and then in the return at Carlton where 10,500 turned up. These crowds were below those usually seen at Australian Rules games, but it was pointed out to us that the Rules season ran in their winter and this was hot summer weather in which the Aussies aren't accustomed to watching football of any code. By then they have turned their attention to cricket.

Meath won all five games: 9 March at Perth against Western Australia by 21 points, 11 March at MCG against Victoria by 11, 13 March under lights at Sydney against New South Wales against a combination of Rules and Gaelic footballers by 17, 15 March in Adelaide against South Australia by 11 again and then the final game, which was a real thriller and very exciting to broadcast, at Carlton against Victoria when the score was 2-9 to 1-7.

It must be said again that the heat was intense for the visitors and it left two lasting memories. One was the sight of the late Father Tully trying to protect his head from the sun by draping a towel Arab-like over himself. During the St Patrick's Day game the ground was so hard and bare of grass that many of the players skinned arms and knees, particularly Bertie Cunningham and Mick Mellett. My wife, Molly, acted as medic administering powder and cream to the cuts. And remember in all this heat I was broadcasting back to Ireland where a few hours later the start of the Railway Cup final at Croke Park between Leinster and Munster was delayed because of blinding hailstones.

* * *

For me the calendar was now punctuated by important dates that never varied and came around, it seemed, with increasing speed. January meant the beginning of the build-up to the Grand National: the publication of the weights always coincided with the Thyestes Chase at Gowran Park. Patrick's Day would see me in Croke Park for the Railway Cup finals and sometimes — depending which day of the week the 17th of March fell on— an inconvenient clash with Cheltenham. Then over to Aintree for the National, back to Fairyhouse for our version of the same, on to Punchestown in May, Epsom in June, the Irish Derby a few weeks later and on through the summer months the tempo intensifying until the twin climaxes of the All-Ireland Finals in September.

It got so hectic I suppose I never thought about the toll it was taking on me and was just swept along with the tide. Two months after returning from Australia I was due to travel to New York for the National Hurling League final between New York and Tipperary on 2 June. The previous fortnight had been particularly busy — a week of show jumping at the White City in London had been followed by racing at the Phoenix Park on Saturday. Something had to give and it did on the day Sir Ivor won the Epsom Derby. I had arranged to fly over the morning of the race and back that evening. By the time I reached Heathrow Airport on the return journey I was feeling very dizzy and wobbly on the legs. When I stumbled on board the air hostess put me lying down across a couple of seats and sent a radio message to have a doctor and an ambulance waiting for me in Dublin.

I was diagnosed as having high blood pressure and after a few weeks in hospital (I missed the Irish Derby that year), I was urged — nay, ordered — to rest for a considerable time. Needless to say there was no trip to New York and RTE Radio had to make abrupt alternative arrangements for the broadcast from Gaelic Park. It so happened that Seán Óg Ó Ceallacháin was in America as a member of the Cushing Games Committee with London footballers who played the Cushing Games at the end of May. On the very day he was due to travel back to Ireland he was contacted by Oonagh Gormley of the Sports Department with the request that he remain in New York for the League final the following Sunday. Ironically that game wasn't played as scheduled as rains began to fall in New York on the Saturday — they had what the Americans call a 'wash out' and it had to be postponed again the following weekend as America was in mourning for Senator Robert Kennedy who had been assassinated in Los Angeles. Eventually the two legs of the League final were staged over the weekend of 15–16 June, with Tipperary winning by 11 points on aggregate, having lost by one on the Saturday evening.

Even though it went against the grain, I had to pass up a whole raft of commentary assignments that summer and indeed, for the first time in my life, I spent the month of August relaxing in Lecanvey. I was back in harness, though, in time to see Wexford hurlers win their fifth All-Ireland and Down their third football crown and I was able to travel to Laurel Park in November to see Lester win the Washington International on Sir Ivor.

Strange experiences in broadcasting? One of the funniest happened in Kilkenny in 1950 — although it seemed anything but funny at the time. The occasion was a Leinster hurling final between Kilkenny and Wexford and there was a huge crowd for Nowlan Park, nearly 37,000, so crushing was severe. The Kilkenny ground wasn't as well equipped then as now and as far as I can recall a radio broadcast had never been done from there previously — those were the times, remember, when radio went around the provinces in the summer with just one commentary each day, not the extensive coverage provided of all championship games when we introduced *Sunday Sport* in the late 1960s. In keeping with the occasion the local committee sought to provide the best vantage point for yours truly and, since they had no permanent commentary box, a saloon car was placed on top of a lorry and situated some way back from the pitch.

This was all right during the minor match, but the bulk of the crowd hadn't arrived at that stage. By the time the big match started I could see only three-quarters of the pitch as the excited crowd on the sideline decided to stand up on the seats thus blotting out my view. With about ten minutes to go in an absolute thriller my view was restricted to about 30 yards, so it was either hand back to the studio or take drastic measures. I decided the match was too good to pass up, so as the engineer, Jack Boyd, waited and watched the 'mike' I clambered up on the roof of the car from where, sitting legs crossed in tailor-like fashion, I continued the commentary.

But what was that grinding sound beneath me? To my horror I discovered that the roof of the car was beginning to cave-in under my weight and I was in danger of collapsing back down into the seats! The day was saved by a friend who was with me and saw what was happening. Being a resourceful fellow he climbed into the car and with his arm outstretched and hand jammed against the roof he kept the commentator in place for the last few minutes!

In this age of satellite television you probably believe there's the absolute in comfort when it comes to American facilities. But not at Gaelic Park, New York and certainly not in the late 1950s when I was there for a St Brendan Cup final between Kerry and New York. It was my first experience of a broadcast from Gaelic Park — all my previous New York commentaries had been from the Polo Grounds and I got a rude shock when I saw that I would be required to work from the end of a 'press box' at sideline level with an open-type microphone. To make matters worse the public address announcements — by one and the same Lefty Devine — were going out over a loudspeaker just over my head. Things were bad enough until the huge crowd on the sideline began moving forward for a better view and then the squad of New York subs — and there weren't just three or four — who had parked themselves in front of me began to move forward also.

At the height of the excitement there was much jumping up and down by these same subs, so there was nothing for it but to decide 'that if you can't beat them, join them.' Luckily the engineer from CBS Radio, who was providing the facilities for me, had a long, long lead on the microphone and I was able to get out in front of spectators and subs. As the game progressed, more and more people moved out onto the sideline and as they moved I moved too until I was broadcasting from well over the line. At one stage Kerry's brilliant right half-back Sean Murphy, came soloing down the wing and I well recall the stunned expression on his face when he caught sight of me several yards out onto the field giving an 'on the spot' description to the listeners at home. In fact, for a moment I thought that in his shock he might pass me the ball!

All a far cry from the old green commentary box which stood in Croke Park for many, many years mounted on 'stilts' and positioned about the centre line between the old Hogan Stand and the Long Stand. I had a very 'soft spot' for that box as it was there that I did my 'audition' commentary and worked from 1938 until it was demolished in 1958 when the erection of the new Hogan Stand began. Although the facilities on the new Hogan are excellent and provide a marvellous view for the commentators I still feel nostalgic about that old green box.

From the very beginning of my career all my broadcasting was 'live' for the simple reason, of course, that there were no recorded commentaries since recording equipment in the 1930s was so very complicated and cumbersome. So having started that way I always preferred live broadcasting and I was never very comfortable with commentaries recorded. Consequently for most of the year — say, October to the end of July — all my commentaries on Gaelic games would be 'live' ones for radio. Then in August, when the All-Ireland series began, I would switch to television for the live telecasts of the semi-finals and finals. Even after I left the full-time staff of RTE in 1972 I had this happy, and for me satisfactory, arrangement of always being involved in live broadcasting. Although no longer Head of Sport I was able to come to this agreement with my successor Fred Cogley, whose compliance I was grateful for. Now that I was no longer Head of the Sports Department at the organisation I was entering a whole new era.

9

Entering A New Era

Gaelic games moved into a new era around the same time as my departure from RTE — although, of course, I cannot say it was in anyway connected with the major change in my career circumstances. Football saw the rise of the new Dubs in the middle of the 1970s, and they and Kerry, who hadn't slipped too far anyhow, dominated the rest of the decade. The Kingdom remained predominant for half of the following decade as well. In hurling, there was a real breath of fresh air when Offaly and Galway broke through the almost total monopoly that had been exerted on the championship by the Cork–Kilkenny–Tipperary axis. All of this meant very, very exciting times for a commentator conveying to listeners or viewers the details of these events as they unfolded.

Dublin's remarkable comeback in 1974 was extraordinary and it brought support for the county's teams to a new level of interest and fanaticism. There had, admittedly, been great support for the Dublin teams of the 1950s, but what happened two decades later hugely surpassed even that. It was, I believe, helped by the more widespread access to television, which wasn't there to cover the Dubs of the 1950s. This new medium, particularly in colour, brought a new dimension to sport everywhere. The stars of foreign soccer teams such as Manchester United, Liverpool, Arsenal and others, together with the sporting personalities of the Olympics were brought right into our living rooms and became household names.

As we went through the 1960s and early 1970s the leading counties in hurling and football all had their own individual heroes who brought their counties additional honours. But not so in Dublin, where the memories of the last All-Ireland football triumph (1963) were fading fast

— and, of course, hadn't been experienced by the youngsters of the city or county. Dublin's lack of success grew into a mounting crisis, it seemed, which led to the frequently-asked question: 'what's wrong with Dublin football?' Indeed, I remember hosting a television discussion one winter's Sunday night, which posed the very same question and sought to get solutions from a panel that, I recall, included the county chairman Jimmy Gray and Kevin Heffernan.

But all that was to change in 1974 and soon Dublin people who hadn't been in Croke Park for years, if ever, were flocking to the national headquarters and to venues all over the country in support of their new idols. A new combination of county colours was adopted for that year's Leinster final against Meath: sky blue with the navy trim and navy shorts instead of the traditional (up to then) sky blue with white trim and white shorts. Soon these jerseys were worn by increasing numbers of supporters replacing the colours of English soccer clubs and indeed, straining the production lines of Paul O'Neill's International sportsgear factory.

But even in our most spectacular dreams we couldn't have envisaged anything like this happening. Certainly not when we went to Croke Park on 26 May that year. The main reason for being there was the replay of the National Football League final between Kerry and Roscommon for which I was providing the radio commentary. I was also reporting on what had happened in the curtain-raiser — the Leinster championship match between Dublin and Wexford. Now just think for a minute: could you nowadays imagine one of Dublin's championship matches being arranged as a curtain-raiser to anything, even a National League final? That's how dramatically things changed in 1974. I won't say that the Dubs were pathetic, but I do recall Kevin Heffernan once saying on a radio programme: 'I remember looking at the second match and saying to myself "My God, it's like the difference there is between men and boys" when I considered what we had produced in the first championship match.'

Of course, quite a lot of the credit for the great changeabout can be attributed to the very same Heffernan. He was the mastermind, a fact acknowledged by everyone connected with the team. I was particularly glad to see his success as a manager this time around, because it was his second time in charge; as productive as his brilliant playing career had been. You see, it was my father, Jim, when chairman of the St Vincent's club and a leading selector, who gave Kevin his first chance on the Vincent's senior team in the late 1940s. That was against St Mary's of Saggart and the young Heffo repaid my dad's confidence in him by scoring a goal.

Dublin had a long way to climb back. Kerry had won the All-Ireland championship as recently as 1969 and 1970 having got over what Jim Brosnan, former star and county chairman, had called their 'seven-year itch' which lasted from the 1962 win over Roscommon to the 1969 success against Offaly. Dublin, on the other hand, hadn't had their hands on the Sam Maguire Cup since 1963. Worse still, they were operating in the lower regions of football — Division 2 of the National League that included several of the counties then classified as the weaker ones, Kilkenny, Limerick, Waterford, Clare and Carlow. In that group the Dubs had been hammered by Clare at Croke Park in February (4-9 to 2-9) and they failed to win the Division 2 title when they were beaten in the final by Kildare — by seven points at Croke Park exactly three weeks before they would commence their successful championship march.

The previous autumn major decisions had been made in both Kerry and Dublin. Gerald McKenna, the chairman in Kerry, had invited Mick O'Dwyer who had played right up to the 1973 Munster final, to take over as manager of the county team. Jimmy Gray, former hurling goalkeeper now in the chair in Dublin, asked Heffernan to return to take charge of Dublin. One of the conditions of Kevin's return was to name his own selectors and he nominated Lorcan Redmond and Donal Colfer, who had never reached the same heights as Heffernan on the field, but who were two individuals whose thinking he knew was in line with his own. Over the next decade Mick and Kevin were to become the principal managerial rivals.

We weren't to know that this was to be the start of something big, a series that would catch the imagination of players all over the country and indeed the imagination of the public as well — and change the very nature of the game.

Heffernan drove home from Croke Park after the first round victory over Wexford thinking about the summer ahead and, immediately, the match against Louth one week later in Navan. In the car with Kevin was a youngster Terry Jennings, who lived close by the Heffernans and whose father Terry had been a team-mate of Heffernan at St

Vincent's. Young Terry regarded Jimmy Keaveney, who had retired from inter-county football 23 months previously, with something approaching hero worship. On the short trip home from Croke Park Terry suggested to Kevin that the manager bring Jimmy back. At the time anyone who might have been listening would have scoffed at the idea because Jimmy was well out of fitness, had put on a lot of weight and on that particular day was so far removed from the Dublin team that he had watched the Dublin-Wexford match from the Hill 16 terraces. But it set Heffernan thinking, he admits, and two days later he persuaded Jimmy to return to the team for the match against Louth.

Heffernan had already put Tony Hanahoe at centre half-forward providing leadership in the attack and detailed to do the additional specific job of opening up opposing defences to provide a channel for attacks to come through. With Keaveney back in the side he now had an acknowledged sharp-shooter available who could turn a good service of the ball into scores. Straightaway Jimmy showed what a valuable asset he could be when he got six points in the defeat of Louth. From there on we saw him bring all his great experience, his natural shrewdness and marksmanship into play and he remained a vital cog in the Dublin machine. At the end of July 1979 a suspension following that year's Leinster final put a second end to his county career. He got two months after being put off in the provincial final, missed the All-Ireland semi-final against Roscommon and was only six days short of making the final against Kerry. As it turned out, the Leinster final with Offaly was his last appearance in the team, but he had already accounted for a goal and 12 points in that year's campaign.

From his comeback in June 1974 until July 1979 Jimmy was the team's prolific scorer and very few equalled, but none bettered, his feats at free-taking. I reckon that in those six championship campaigns of the 1970s he was responsible for 13 goals and 162 points of Dublin's accumulative tally.

The amazing turn around in Dublin's fortunes was completed when they carried off the Sam Maguire Cup in September with a victory in the final over Galway when Paddy Cullen made that dramatic save from Liam Sammon's penalty shot. Liam was acknowledged as one of the best penalty-takers of the time and I must confess I expected him to score from the spot as he stepped up to this important kick with

Galway just a point ahead 12 minutes into the second half. He kicked right, Cullen moved to his left and I still remember shouting: 'He's saved it, oh!, he's saved it!'

Meanwhile down in Kerry Mick O'Dwyer was reorganising the forces. A lot of the players who appeared in the 1974 Munster final against Cork were players Mick himself had figured with on the team, so he recognised the difficulty he would have coming in as manager with so many of his recent team-mates under him. So a definite decision was made by himself and the other selectors to concentrate on younger players. He saw the high level of fitness Heffernan had attained with the Dublin squad and he knew it would have to be a priority for Kerry to be equally fit, if not fitter, if they were to get back the Sam Maguire Cup in 1975. He had the squad of players who were willing to put in the supreme effort to achieve this objective. Among those brought into the team were Jimmy Deenihan, Tim Kennelly, Ogie Moran and Pat Spillane, Paidí Ó Sé, Mike Sheehy, Ger Power and John Egan.

Probably not many people in Kerry expected this reconstructed team to get to the All-Ireland final so quickly; O'Dwyer was certainly confident that they would. It was a great confrontation between two great rivals, who hadn't met in the final since 1955 when Heffernan as full-forward had experienced the deep disappointment of defeat. There were great expectations: again the classic clash between the city slickers and the county that represented all that was best in the country cousins.

It was so eagerly awaited and interest in the meeting was extraordinary. One other feature of this final: it was probably the first championship in which videotape was extensively used in the teams' preparations. Of course home video recorders were becoming more and more common and team officials were recording the live telecasts, but now we had county teams getting cameramen to cover their games. Kevin Heffernan especially used this as a means of getting his players to look back on their performances.

From the start his friend, Tiernan McBride, recorded all Dublin's matches, especially those which wouldn't be covered by RTE and the tapes were subsequently viewed by the players after training sessions. O'Dwyer also used videos. 'Dublin,' he later said, 'were an exceptionally fit side, we watched them on video and what have you, and we decided that there was only one way to take them on and that was to get our team exceptionally fit, so we trained very hard. We trained 28 consecutive days for that final.'

Dublin were the champions and favourites, but they were rattled very soon after the start when Mike Sheehy caused some confusion in the Dublin defence that led to a third minute goal. The free from about 35 yards out dropped short instead of sailing over the bar as Mike's frees usually did and John Egan was on the spot to slam it into the net. Kerry never looked back and they won fairly easily by seven points. The game provided the unusual occurrence of a captain who didn't know he was the captain until just before going up for the Sam Maguire Cup. You see, Mickey Sullivan, who led Kerry into the final, had been injured in a clash with full-back Sean Doherty after 20 minutes and was in hospital with concussion by the time the match finished. So Pat Spillane went up to get the trophy, but he was told only when the game finished that he was the captain.

Pat was still a couple of months short of his 20th birthday at the time and he recalled: 'I wasn't told until after the game because Mickey got injured just before half-time. The selectors didn't like to tell me at half-time that I was the captain because it might affect my game. Obviously it would because I was too young.'

That led to an epic series of clashes, one of the most exciting that football has ever known. The two counties dominated the sport for the rest of the 1970s and were continuously meeting each other. Consequently there was remarkable interest in each game, never more so than when they clashed again 12 months later in the 1976 final.

In the meantime Dublin had got a new half-back line with Tommy Drumm and Kevin Moran coming into the side and Pat O'Neill returning. It was young Moran who provided us with a spectacular move in the very early seconds; full of self-confidence and unabashed by the great tradition behind Kerry, Kevin swept upfield on a daring, cheeky run with the ball. He got way beyond midfield and I remember wondering how he could be allowed solo so far. And he wasn't finished yet. He passed the ball to midfielder Bernard Brogan and kept going for the return pass before kicking a screaming shot just inches the wrong side of the post. It would have been the most sensational goal to be scored in an All-Ireland final, but the irony of it is that it is still one of the best remembered incidents from a final despite the fact that Kevin had kicked a wide.

As it turned out it was a wide Dublin could afford because Jimmy Keaveney, John McCarthy and Brian Mullins had a goal each and the defence restricted the Kerry forwards to points. So it was a comprehensive win for the Dubs, who could now hold their heads high and smile at the taunts that had been thrown at them over the previous two years, especially when they won the championship in 1974, that they had never beaten Kerry.

Eleven months later the All-Ireland championship sequence brought them together in the semi-final. For me, and I suspect, for many, many people, the very best game between them was that 1977 semi-final. It was a contest of enormous proportions, with two super-fit teams playing at an astonishing pace; tough at times with the referee Seamus Murray 'booking' a few players but the action never came near boiling point. The football was fluent, adventurous, thoughtful and constructive with the play swinging up and down the field constantly. It was the sort of game that tests the tonsils of a commentator; a match you dream about seeing, but only rarely come across.

It fluctuated tensely. Kerry ahead at half-time by a goal, back level by the 39th minute after John McCarthy got a Dublin goal — and they had missed two that we thought would destroy them in the first half. Bernard Brogan, back from France where he was working, was brought into midfield and he and Mullins lorded it in an area where Kerry were traditionally the masters. Scores were equal more than once, but in the 56th minute Dublin took the lead for the first time in the match. In this extraordinary battle they were not only caught, but headed again by Kerry who went two in front with just less than ten minutes left. But then the semi-final turned on two incidents. Brian Mullins sent a sideline kick to Anton O'Toole who passed to Hanahoe, next a deflection from John O'Keeffe and the ball fell to David Hickey who was through for a goal. Then Pat O'Neill launched an attack and Brogan went charging through the middle before being set up by Hanahoe for another.

That, though, was the end of Dublin's victories over Kerry. From there on Kerry were really on top. Seanie Walsh joined Jack O'Shea in midfield, Paidí Ó Sé had moved to the half-back line and Ger Power up into the attack and Eoin Liston, the big targetman, had been introduced to full-forward. I suppose not many of us truly realised it at the time, but we were seeing the formation of the greatest football side the sport had known. There will be other contenders, of course, mainly depending on the claimants' county loyalties, but Kerry's record incontrovertibly stands the test. Over a 12-year period the county appeared in ten All-Ireland finals and lost only two: 1976 to Dublin and 1982 to Offaly. Of course, it wasn't entirely the same team from 1975 to 1986, but it was a period in which they produced a team of scintillating skills, developed unbelievably dazzling team-work and discovered new depths of resourcefulness with backs attacking and attackers frequently back defending. It was total football played with utter dedication and with an almost monastic devotion to Mick O'Dwyer's training methods.

By the time the 1978 final came along Kerry were motivated to a very high degree and many of them will tell you that it all started on a very wet day in New York's Gaelic Park where they played very, very well against Dublin in a charity match. They were smarting from the disappointments of 1976 and 1977 and set their hearts during that trip to America on the All-Ireland championship — Dublin or no Dublin.

The final of 1978 was remarkable for a number of reasons. Kevin Moran came over from Manchester United with permission from their manager Dave Sexton to play in the game, but he was injured in training during the week at Parnell Park and he restarted the second half with a heavily bandaged thigh. Then he cut his forehead and played on with a blood-soaked head bandage, but couldn't save Dublin from a hammering. The amazing thing is that the Dubs were almost totally in control in the first 25 minutes, led by five points and were so much in command that even corner backs Gay O'Driscoll and Robbie Kelleher were advancing on the attack. Maybe that was the start of their troubles. The whole team was so attack-minded that they left themselves wide open and soon John Egan was in to handpass a goal (yes, handpassed goals were allowed in those days!).

Now we had the incident for which this final will probably be clearly remembered long after everything else in the game is forgotten; the incident which Paddy Cullen refers to as 'That Goal.' Paddy had fouled Ger Power who had come chasing in as the goalkeeper cleared the ball. The referee, Seamus Aldridge, didn't see it, but the spectators did and they kept barracking Paddy afterwards. Then these two clashed again in almost the same spot out to the left of the large 'square' at the canal end goal. Paddy believes they 'just brushed shoulders' but this time the ref gave a free to Kerry. Cullen was still protesting to Seamus when Robbie Kelleher handed the ball to Mike Sheehy, who took a quick free and lobbed the ball over Cullen's head into the net.

The final of 1979 was utterly onesided with Jack O'Shea and Seanie Walsh dominant at midfield. Kerry had to start without Ger Power, they lost John O'Keeffe with an injury during the game and Paidí Ó Sé was ordered off for a second booking, yet the numerically reduced Kerry could still win by double scores (22 points to 11) 3-13 to 1-8. It was the Kerry team at the height of their powers and in full flow and it was to be the last major meeting with Dublin for a time because the following year Offaly took over in Leinster and it was then Kerry versus Offaly for a short period.

Even now the Kerry players probably won't want to be reminded of that Offaly team. In 1981 the Kingdom completed a sequence of four consecutive titles, something which Wexford (1915–'18) and Kerry (1929–'32) had previously achieved, but nobody had done the five-in-a-row, so Kerry were all the more determined going into the 1982 championship. With their vast experience, and superb record, they were hot favourites to win again and create this new record. But that final disastrous moment (for Kerry, that is) still often replays in my mind. Kerry were two points up with hardly more than a minute left when Richie Connor passed to full-back Liam Connor who came charging downfield (who let him?) and lobbed a ball slightly to the left of the Kerry 'square' where Seamus Darby, who had been sent into attack (in desperation?) by Eugene McGee, outjumped Tommy Doyle before lashing his kick high to the net. Offaly were champions and no five-in-a-row!

It took Kerry two years to get back. Of course the Centenary Year All-Ireland championship in 1984 stood out like a beacon for them. Having won so many titles, and led the roll of honour for so many decades, they felt it was their 'right' to win this centenary championship. All of them were dedicated to giving it 'one last go' for this very special year and here again was the classic meeting with Dublin. But Kerry rose to it once again with magnificent resolve against the All-Ireland champions and 'one last go' seemed very premature when they went on to win the 1985 title with another victory over Dublin and then had another three-in-a-row when they beat Tyrone in 1986.

But it was the clashes of the 1970s we will remember most: four All-Ireland finals, a semi-final and the 1977 National League final with Kerry winning all of them except the 1976 final and that great 1977 semi-final. Perhaps the feature that was most noteworthy about this whole era was the spirit in which the games were played. The rivalry was intense — the urban versus rural element increasing the hype — and, of course, there were some tempestuous moments, but they were very, very few. The teams respected each other immensely and friendships were developed. Certainly there was no bitterness; nothing like that which marred the Cork-Meath games in the late 1980s.

Mick O'Dwyer has said: 'They were the best games we had: National League games, tournament games or in the championship they were great games. And the amazing part of it all was that both sides went out there to play football. They beat us well in '76 and we beat them well in the All-Irelands of '78 and '79 but there was great football in all those games: I don't think anybody can deny that. I think it was always the ambition that Dublin was the team you wanted to beat and the team they wanted to beat was Kerry, and all the sweeter if it was in the All-Ireland final. Agreement from Kevin Heffernan, who stated: 'I think a Kerry All-Ireland won against Dublin is worth two others to them and certainly it's worth three to us to beat Kerry in the final. I enjoy Kerry people and the craic that goes on between Dubliners and Kerry people very much. We have, I think, an almost unique relationship.'

And I say: isn't that what sport is all about?

* * *

The new era in hurling was launched, not by counties who had a background of traditional championship rivalry like Kerry and Dublin, but by teams such as Offaly and Galway, who brought hurling onto a new plane in the 1980s. They were keen enough rivals because they were neighbours across the Shannon and the competitive element between them was nowhere more noticeably underlined than in the Banagher area where Galway begins the minute you cross the halfway point on the bridge over the river.

For years and years the championships had almost been monopolised by Cork, Kilkenny and Tipperary. Indeed, Offaly and Galway very frequently appeared to be no more than easy fodder to feed the ravenous appetites of the Big Three. Both were counties starved of success in hurling, but at least Galway — through their unique situation without realistic opposition in Connacht — had appeared in some All-Ireland finals over the decades, but Offaly hadn't even had the experience of getting to one. Nor, in fact, had they even the pleasure of winning the Leinster championship, so what happened to them in the 1980s and since is all the more remarkable and welcome. Needless to say on a personal level I've been delighted because of relatives and friends I've had in the county: remember, my mother moved from Clare at a very early age and she was reared in Tullamore so my connections with Offaly go very deep.

There was also my friendship with John Dowling and my knowledge of the sterling work of John and many others, notably people like the late Sean Robbins in Birr, Rody O'Brien, Br Denis, and Michael Verney among them and, of course, in modern times Andy Gallagher and Mick Spain. They were tireless in their efforts to take Offaly to glory in the world of hurling, but their resources were very limited. It wasn't fully realised, and still isn't, that the real hurling areas of the county hardly extend much beyond a 10–15 mile radius of Birr. Effectively it's like having two counties, football in two-thirds of it with hurling in the other third.

Now Offaly are truly established as a real hurling power, but in their delight at this situation some of the county's supporters, with the great help of hindsight, are inclined at times to scoff at the scepticism expressed at the beginning of the 1980s by sports journalists, especially those in newspapers, writing previews of the big matches. As they went into the 1980 Leinster final against Kilkenny they were not highly rated against the then All-Ireland champions. It was the county's first appearance in the provincial final since 1969, and indeed only their fifth in all, and what some Offaly people now forget is that the vast majority of them appeared to have a shared disbelief that they could stop Kilkenny because only 9,613 people turned up for that

Michael and American commentator Lefty Devine at Gaelic Park, New York.

Lefty Devine makes a presentation to Molly in Gaelic Park, New York.

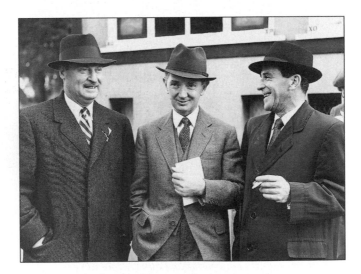

S. J. Perlman, Vincent O'Brien and John Schapiro.

Commentating with the family. Michael, Tony, Molly and Michael Jr.

Inspecting the course with Peter O'Sullevan.

Michael in 1950.

*Discussing the Belmont card with one of his American opposite numbers,
Fred Capossela.*

At Belmont Park in the 1950s.

Irish journalists in the Gresham Hotel with John Schapiro, Tony Power, Tony Sweeney, Louis Gunning, Mick Byrne, Paul McWeeney, Vaughan Briscoe, Frank Hall, Gerry Merren and Sean Murphy.

Talking to John Schapiro, Liverpool, 1951.

With trainer Paddy Murphy and racing journalist Christy Glennon.

Compèring the gala opening of RTE.

Travelling with Meath in Australia, March 1968.

Singing in the rain?

Sean Ó Siocháin, Cearbhall Ó Dálaigh, Rev. Br. O'Connor and Michael.

Tom Hardiman, Director General of RTE, presents Michael with the cartoon (next page) on his retirement as Head of Sport.

RTE's farewell present to Michael, 1972.

Inspecting Becher's Brook. From left to right: Colman Doyle, Billy Merriman, Michael and Eddie McDonnell.

Meeting the Queen Mother.

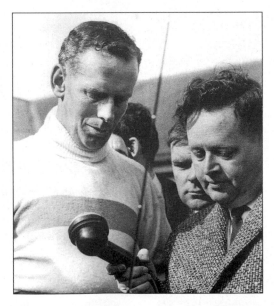

With jockey Pat Taaffe at Fairyhouse, 1964.

Interviewing Liam Ward in 1970.

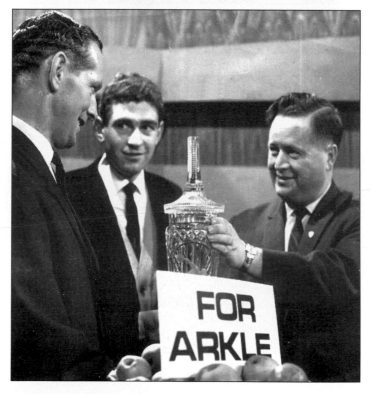

Presenting Pat Taaffe with the RTE Sportsman of the Year Award.
Johnny Lumley, Arkle's lad, stands in the centre.

High above Epsom in the NBC hot air balloon.

Calling the colours.

Paul McWeeney, Mitchel Cogley and Michael in the 1970s.

*Paddy Buggy, President of the GAA, makes a Centenary Year
presentation to Michael in 1984.*

The family gathers.

At Croke Park with Peter.

Leinster final on 13 July, 1980. That was more than 16,000 lower than the average provincial hurling final crowd over the previous five years and the first time it dipped below 10,000 in living memory. But the lack of faith displayed even by their own didn't upset the players and they had a marvellous victory in a very high-scoring game — 3-17 to 5-10. From long-serving goalkeeper Damien Martin down to left full-forward, two-goal Johnny Flaherty, another great veteran, this exuberant team showed that Offaly were on the way. And things would never be the same again in hurling.

Nobody who knew about Offaly hurling would say it was a sudden change — the groundwork had been laid for quite some time. But it was certainly dramatic. Looking back now we can see just how dramatic. As I've said, for decades Offaly couldn't even get to the Leinster final — only four in the 91 championship years prior to 1980. Then they couldn't be kept out of the decider for more than a decade: from 1980 to 1990 inclusive they played in every Leinster final, which was a wonderful record of consistency. Not only that but they were then also capable of reaching All-Ireland finals. First they had to encounter Galway and suffer the disappointment of defeat in the semi-final of 1980, but they were back again the following year and met Galway again. There was added piquancy to all of this because of the Banagher connection: some of the Galway players would have attended the vocational school in Banagher and actually played for Offaly in vocational schools' competitions.

Galway had, as the cliché puts it, ploughed a lone furrow for many decades and even when they went into the Munster championship for a period (1959–'70) they were unable to make a breakthrough. They suffered some very humiliating defeats, the most recent a loss to Kilkenny in 1975 by 11 points — the first 70-minute final — and again in 1979 when beaten by seven points. But suddenly everything changed: a year later they were All-Ireland champions after a lapse of 56 years having previously won the title in 1924 in the delayed 1923 final.

Sometimes it's surprising what you remember about a game — and what you don't recall, even about an All-Ireland final. Two great memories stand-out in my mind from Galway's victory in that final over Limerick. Not the goals by Bernie Forde and P.J. Molloy, nor Limerick's three by Eamonn Cregan (2) and Joe McKenna, but the wonderful scenes at the end as Galway's captain Joe Connolly turned the presentation into a truly memorable occasion. For years we've had to suffer some forgettable, cliché-ridden 'speeches' by winning captains, but here for once we had a marvellous and passionate outpouring of pent-up emotion, The scene was somewhat reminiscent of the post-match celebrations after Down's win in 1960, but no one had matched Joe's speech. He remembered the bad old days, he spoke to Galway people all over the world and it was mostly all in the Irish which is the first language of his great family. He finished with the stirring exclamation: 'People of Galway we love you!'

Then there was the sight of such great veterans as Joe's older brother John and P.J. Molloy going onto the presentation dais. John Connolly, at 32 about to get his first All-Ireland medal as a result of this win, had experienced the worst of times with Galway, but had been a great servant of hurling since joining the county senior team 13 years previously. Never before had he experienced a moment of celebration such as this.

Come to think of it, it isn't exactly accurate to say that Galway's breakthrough was sudden. Because earlier that year there had been omens, which we might have paid better attention to if we weren't blinded by tradition. On St Patrick's Day their team representing Connacht had won the Railway Cup by beating Munster. At the end of May, Castlegar, their county champions with six Connollys actually appearing on the field at one stage of the final, won the All-Ireland club championship by beating one of the Cork Big Three, Blackrock.

The trainer/selector to the team was Cyril Farrell who was to become much better known before the end of the decade for his immense contribution to Galway hurling as their manager. No more than a club hurler, Cyril had an unshakeable belief in Galway hurling and he had no time for the defeatist attitude that so frequently had afflicted various Galway teams over the years when facing the more successful counties from Munster and Leinster. Starting with minors and under-21s Cyril, as much as any other person, turned Galway into winners and enabled them to grow in self-confidence.

Something similar had happened in Offaly at the turn of the decade. They had taken advice from friends in Kilkenny and sent out an invitation to Dermot Healy, who had some notable success with Kilkenny minor teams. He was dubious about taking over, but eventually did and had his first meeting with the players after a National League match in Birr early in November 1979. In his role as coach he worked with trainer/manager Andy Gallagher and helped to change Offaly from being a potentially good but very physical team into one of supreme skill. They worked on their great spirit and dedication to the game of hurling. It could be said that Healy convinced Offaly that they could win an All-Ireland final, having first made a major breakthrough by winning the Leinster final in 1980.

When Offaly got through to the final in 1981 against Galway, tradition, it appeared, was against them for the history of hurling showed that teams didn't win the championship in their first appearance in the final. But then blowing tradition out the window was nothing to this team — in more recent years Derry and Donegal have taken the football title at the first attempt but in hurling it has always been harder because hurling could, in a sense, be looked on as a sort of closed shop for the few. For a long time it seemed Offaly wouldn't do it, as Galway, with Joe Connolly superbly accurate from frees, actually led by eight points five minutes into the second half. Galway then missed chances and a storming comeback for Offaly was launched when Aidan Fogarty and Pat Delaney swopped places on the half-back line and Padraig Horan and Johnny Flaherty did the same on the full-forward line.

So Galway and Offaly had made their impact on the sport with these wins and it was underlined with further victories in the 1980s. In fact, between them they took half of the titles in that decade: Galway three and Offaly two. Perhaps even more important, the solid work being done for the game in both counties saw them also having success at under-21 and minor level as well — Galway winning their first minor in 1983, Offaly doing so three years later and again in 1987 and '89. Galway now has under-21 titles as well, while Offaly has reached All-Ireland finals at this level, so the future is indeed bright. Never again can any county take either of these two teams for granted as has happened in so much of history.

They were to meet in another final and two semi-finals before the decade was out. Offaly won in 1985 in the final and in the 1984 semi-final, but Galway won in 1988. By the middle of the decade the younger set had come along in both counties — in Offaly John Troy, Mark and Paddy Corrigan, Joachim Kelly and Joe Dooley, and in

Galway that outstanding half-back line of Peter Finnerty, Tony Keady and Gerry McInerney as well as Joe Cooney and Eanna Ryan in the attack — and we saw some super and elegant hurling. Perhaps, though the biggest disappointment for Offaly was in the Centenary All-Ireland final held in Thurles. That was a stirring occasion, superbly and efficiently organised despite the doubting Thomases who had predicted chaos, and it was a great day to be in Semple Stadium. For Cork, but not for Offaly. Cork swept through the game, as they have so often on the famous sod, and won easily by ten points.

Having won their first All-Ireland hurling championship in 1981 Offaly just missed recording a double two weeks later when they were beaten by Kerry in the football decider; Liam Currams, the 20-year-old from Kilcormac who was at midfield in hurling and left half-back at football, just failed to become the first player ever to win the two medals in one year — something which Teddy McCarthy of Cork achieved in 1990. Of course, Offaly got the football success a year later — sorry Kerry! there we go reminding you again of the five-in-a-row that never was — but their disappointment in 1981 shouldn't take from the county's achievements in the 1980s. Realistically in modern times we don't expect any county but Cork to be in contention for the double — Galway with a very, very outside chance and Dublin in other decades maybe when their hurling was stronger than the football. But Offaly achieved what no other county of their size or with their relatively limited population has done — they played in five All-Ireland finals in the 1980s, three hurling and two football, and won three out of the five.

The extraordinary thing about this dual success was the contribution made by two men from outside the county: Dermot Healy in hurling and Eugene McGee in football. Eugene had been tremendously successful in the 1970s when he was in charge of the UCD team that won club All-Irelands, but he had no experience at county level. However he was a superb organiser and he set out telling the players at the start that he had no intention of trying to outdo Kerry and Dublin at the short-passing game.

A native of Longford, he said later: 'I think that came as a bit of a shock to them because at that stage if you didn't play handpassing football you were supposed to be backward or thick or ignorant. I had to get across to them that we were going to change and try and bring back the catch and the long kicking as the fundamental components of the Offaly game. In fairness to the players they quickly grasped it.'

They were so successful at it that it is now sad to see how Offaly football has slumped since the mid-1980s. The county still remains at the forefront in hurling and, thankfully, that's also the case in Galway. But at football Offaly has faded as a power and you'd wonder what is the explanation when they are still such a force at hurling?

10

BBC Calling

As equine personalities go, Prince Regent was up there with the very best. The star of Tom Dreaper's stable was the Arkle of his time, quite simply the best chaser in Ireland. Unfortunately his peak years coincided with the Second World War and it was not until normality returned that Dreaper was able to let the British racing public see how good he was by entering him for both the 1946 Cheltenham Gold Cup and the Grand National.

The horse's fame had preceded him, of course, which is why I, as the voice of racing on Radio Éireann, was invited to join the BBC commentary team for the Gold Cup. Perched on a platform down the course I watched with patriotic pride as Tim Hyde put the Prince through his paces. Just for a moment my heart was in my mouth when not far from my position the horse's feet slipped on a turn and almost went from under him. Happily he quickly recovered and galloped over his five rivals to win by five lengths.

A highly significant sequel to that Gold Cup broadcast came in the form of a telegram addressed to:

> O'HEHIR PLOUGH HOTEL CHELTENHAM.

It read:

> MANY THANKS FOR CHELTENHAM BROADCAST STOP THOUGHT COMMENTARY WENT EXCELLENT STOP WOULD YOU UNDERTAKE GRAND NATIONAL COMMENTARY AT CANAL TURN STOP

Would I what!

The telegram was from S. J. Lotbiniere, Head of Outside Broadcasts at the BBC.

124

So it was back to England a few weeks later to begin my love affair with 'the greatest steeplechase in the world' that lasted until 1984. My co-commentators on that first occasion were the incomparable Peter O'Sullevan and Raymond Glendenning.

The speculation in the lead-up to that year's race was all about Prince Regent. He was being asked to shoulder 12 st 5 lb round the famous course, a much tougher test in those days than it was to become in later years. Nevertheless he was made the warm 3-to-1 favourite to beat a field of 35. Three fences from home I was convinced he was going to do it. As I handed over to Glendenning in the Grandstand he was ten lengths clear and going well, but unfortunately, he had been bothered by loose horses all the way round and Tim Hyde had used up all his speed to keep him clear of the trouble. In any event they had no answer when Lovely Cottage came with a storming run from the second last. Close home Prince Regent was caught by Jack Finlay and relegated to third place.

It was truly a brave performance by certainly the best chaser sent out of Ireland until Arkle came along. Indeed, old Tom Dreaper used to maintain that Prince Regent was every bit as good as Arkle although towards the end of his life he was prepared to concede he might be wrong on that score.

The annual pilgrimage to Cheltenham and Liverpool became an important part of my working life as did the many hours spent pouring over form books and memorising colours, especially coming up to Aintree. Two years after my BBC debut I was privileged to broadcast and report on Cottage Rake's first Gold Cup which I described in the next day's *Irish Independent* as 'a great feather in the cap of that fine Munster trainer, Vincent O'Brien.'

This is how Vincent remembers his first trip to Cheltenham: 'I led Cottage Rake out on the course and decided to go down to the last fence to watch the race. As they came to the last Martin Molony on Happy Home jumped it a length and a half clear of Aubrey Brabazon on Cottage Rake. There was no public address in those days and there was no use asking anybody around what had won. I made my way towards the unsaddling enclosure by way of the back of the stands and at this stage I dared not ask anybody what won. I was holding on to my wildest hopes. As I approached the winner's enclosure Cottage Rake was coming from the opposite direction and I saw Aubrey touching his cap.

The greatest moment of my life had just become a reality.' There were to be many more such days I would share with Vincent and rejoice in his success.

The following year he went to Cheltenham with a much stronger hand. On the Tuesday he saddled Hatton's Grace to win the first of his three Champion Hurdles. Dubbed by me 'the ugly duckling of the parade ring', Hatton's Grace had once changed hands for 18 guineas but he pulverised the opposition that day to win by six lengths. On the Wednesday Castledermot completed a double for the O'Brien stable by winning the National Hunt Chase (known as the Amateurs' Grand National), in the hands of the famous Lord Mildmay.

That night the weather turned nasty and the third day of the meeting was called off. This was a blessing in disguise for Vincent because Cottage Rake had been held up in his Gold Cup preparation by a lingering cold and runny nose so the horse had an extra month to get fit for what was to be the toughest race of his life. Coming to the last the Rake was two lengths behind Cool Customer but there was no cooler a customer around that day than jockey Aubrey Brabazon, and how the champion responded to his urging, flying up the hill to win one of the greatest Gold Cup races by two lengths. As I wrote at the time, 'Cottage Rake was turned out an equine masterpiece by O'Brien'.

Eleven months later Irish cheers rang out again to greet Cottage Rake's hat trick of Gold Cups. It was the easiest of the three: he won by ten lengths, not breathing hard.

> *'Aubrey's up, the money's down*
> *The frightened bookies quake,*
> *Come on, me lads, and give a cheer*
> *Begod, 'tis Cottage Rake.'*

Two days earlier Hatton's Grace, with victories in the Irish Lincoln and Cesarewitch behind him, had retained the Champion Hurdle title, a feat he was to repeat in 1951, with Tim Molony in the saddle instead of Brabazon. It all made great copy for an Irish racing journalist. Still to come, of course, perhaps the most amazing of all O'Brien's amazing achievements: three Grand Nationals in a row.

* * *

After Mr Joe Griffin ('Mincemeat Joe') had led in the winner of the Grand National for the second year in succession on 27 March, 1954, he announced to the world that his ambition was to win the greatest steeplechase in the world again the next year. But ten months later Joe was in the Bankruptcy Court and his two National winners, Early Mist and Royal Tan, were under new ownership.

To go back to the beginning of this stranger-than-fiction story, when millionaire J. V. Rank died in 1952, his dream of winning the National unfulfilled, his horses were sold at the Curragh on Irish Derby Day. One of them, Early Mist, a faller in that year's National, was knocked down to Vincent O'Brien for 5,300 guineas. He bought it on behalf of a new patron, Mr Griffin, a Dublin businessman who had made a substantial fortune in the post-World War II years.

Early Mist was difficult to train because of a splint in his foreleg. Nevertheless after three inauspicious preparatory races in the spring of 1953 O'Brien had him ready for Aintree. I was not so sure. Three weeks before the big race I was working at Hurst Park when word came through that Early Mist had won at Naas but had been disqualified. I tried to cancel my ante-post bet on the National but happily the bookmaking firm would not agree.

O'Brien had booked Bryan Marshall, a jockey he greatly admired, for the Aintree race, and this superb horseman steered clear of all trouble to win 'in a common canter' as reported at the time. Marshall's comment to me afterwards was that Early Mist was 'still a baby'.

'Mincemeat' Joe was overjoyed, needless to say, but little did I know what the future held when I opened my report in the *Irish Independent* with these words: 'No matter what fortune may come the way of Dublin businessman Mr J. H. Griffin I doubt if ever again he will experience the supreme thrill reflected in his face when he led in Early Mist.' Early Mist had started at 20 to 1 and Griffin boasted that the race had netted him £30,000: £20,000 on bets and £10,000 in stake money. Some of it went on wild celebrations, first at the Adelphi Hotel in Liverpool, and a few days later in Dublin when the Aintree winner was paraded from Parnell Monument to the Mansion House, there to be received by the Lord Mayor, Senator Clarkin. When Early Mist finally made it home to Tipperary the bands were out and the streets of Cashel were decorated.

Twelve months later I was writing in the *Independent*: 'To win the Grand National as an owner, trainer and jockey is an achievement; to win it two years running with different horses is something akin to a miracle.'

Royal Tan had been O'Brien's very first Grand National runner, back in 1951. Originally owned by Ben Dunne — founder of Dunnes Stores — he was bought by the Keoghs of Knock Hard and Hattons's Grace fame, with the idea of winning the 1950 National Hunt Chase at Cheltenham. Ridden by Vincent's brother, Phonsie, he started favourite but fell at the second fence.

A year later, in the space of ten days, Phonsie rode the seven-year-old in both the Irish and English Nationals and finished second each time. The Aintree race was chaotic, hardly any of the 36 runners getting round without mishap. Going to the last the race was between Royal Tan and Johnny Bullock's mount Nickel Coin. Phonsie shouted over to Bullock 'What are you on?' and added 'I have you goosed anyway', or words to that effect. Unfortunately Royal Tan hit the last, and went right down on his nose. Phonsie managed to stay on but their chance of winning was gone. In 1952 the same thing happened. Royal Tan was lying close up in third place when he stumbled over the last and this time Phonsie could not stay in the saddle.

The horse was out of action for 18 months after that with leg trouble and by the time the 1954 National came round he had been sold by the Keoghs to Joe Griffin who wanted a runner to take the place of Early Mist, then side-lined with injury.

Bryan Marshall rode him in his final warm-up race, the Thyestes Chase at Gowran Park, and was unceremoniously unseated at the open ditch. O'Brien was worried that the horse and rider were not getting on so he arranged a special schooling session after racing at the next Gowran Park meeting and instructed Marshall to let the horse jump the fences his own way. Marshall sat still as a mouse and the horse jumped perfectly. 'Now I've got it,' he said, grinning.

So to Aintree and one of the most exciting Nationals in all my years. Royal Tan was in front between the last two fences. He jumped his bogey fence perfectly but all the way up the straight was challenged by Tudor Line and George Slack. Royal Tan got there by a neck and O'Brien said afterwards: 'When the two horses were racing neck and neck down the finishing straight I was very much aware I had the best jockey in the world on Royal Tan.'

One side-light of that National has stuck in my mind. A next door neighbour of mine, a young woman, drew Royal Tan in the Sweep and was about to sell a half share for £500 until I stepped in and arranged a much better deal. She got £2,500 for the half share and travelled over to Liverpool to see Royal Tan net her ten times that again for the half share she kept. My present was a pair of slippers stamped '33/6' (thirty-three shillings and sixpence).

By now, the Grand National had become something of an obsession with Vincent O'Brien and the next year he mounted a four-pronged attack on the race: his two previous winners, Early Mist and Royal Tan, now belonging respectively to Mr John Dunlop and Prince Aly Khan, along with Oriental Way, to be ridden by Fred Winter, and a newcomer to Aintree, Quare Times, for whom he engaged Pat Taaffe. I remember on the eve of the race Pat telling me that Vincent had had all four jockeys — himself, Winter (Oriental Way), Marshall (Early Mist) and Dave Dick (Royal Tan) up to his room and showed them films of the last four Grand Nationals, pointing out where and how horses had come to grief. It was an early demonstration of the thoroughness that was to become the O'Brien hallmark. On the day it was the weather that almost ruined everything.

The rain lashed down and the course was so wet it was touch and go whether the race would take place. The Queen was there so it did go on, though the water jump was cut out. For Royal Tan, carrying 12 st 4 lb and Early Mist, 12 st 3 lb, the ankle deep mud was too much, though both got round finishing twelfth and ninth, respectively. Oriental Way was knocked over by a falling horse at the eleventh but nothing got in the way of Quare Times and Taaffe. They sailed over all the fences and hacked up 20 lengths ahead of Tudor Line and George Slack, the combination that had run Royal Tan so close the year before.

The name Quare Times did not, as some of the English uppercrust thought, derive from the Latin. The horse, in fact, was called after a famous greyhound owned by Bill Quinn of Killenaule and in the National ran in the colours of Mrs Cecily Welman, who lived near Mullingar. Great was the rejoicing when the victorious party got back to Westmeath. A crowd of 7,000 people and two bands turned out in the streets of Mullingar to greet the horse, the trainer and the jockey. Ah, those were the days!

* * *

'How are you able to identify so many horses, racing so quickly and so close together, is it their numbers?'

A question that has been asked of me, and, no doubt, of most other racing commentators so many times over the years. For obvious reasons, the knack of identifying horses at speed cannot be based on their numbercloths. The job is all about identifying the jockey's colours and it is only when there are similarities in colours, and shades of colours, that other factors — the colour of the horse, blinkers, noseband and bandages — come into the equation.

Mention a racehorse's name to your average racegoer and the chances are he, or she, will tell you something about the animal's form, who trains or owns the horse or maybe the breeding of the animal, if pedigrees are the particular individual's strong-point.

You might be told how much the racegoer has lost on the horse in question or how it would 'definitely have won if the so and so jockey had been able to ride', but very rarely you will hear 'red, black hoop, striped sleeves and a yellow cap' or any other description of racing colours for that matter.

Calling the Horses, as my colleague and long-time friend Peter O'Sullevan titled his autobiography, is all about colours and the ability to quickly put a horse's name against a particular set. Mention a horse's name to any commentator and it is long odds on the first thing that will spring to his mind is the owner's colours.

Problems arise when the same owner has more than one horse running in a race. When that happens, the Clerk of the Scales, the person who weighs out the jockeys for each race, requests a change of cap colour.

With the colours logged away and the help of a photographic memory, the commentator is half way there.

In many ways, learning the race commentary trade is similar to a schoolchild doing homework the old-fashioned way. It is all about repetition. Not four and four equals eight or five and five equals ten. But red, black hoop and cap, equals Dawn Run, green and yellow hoops, white cap equals Jack Of Trumps, etc. Having learned the basics, there are other factors to be considered and many pitfalls to try and avoid. The siting of the commentary box, the size of the actual racecourse and the weather, so often the bane of a commentator's life.

Don't believe for one minute that all the problems are caused by rain or fog. Such conditions can create a nightmare scenario. But, strange as it might seem, the sun can be an even bigger headache. Ask anyone who has called a race over the straight mile or the seven furlong course at The Curragh when the sun is shining or when it is low in the sky casting shadows in the distance. In the autumn races on the round course at the Curragh can be equally difficult for the same reasons. This problem has been all the more prevalent since the arrival of starting stalls in Ireland in the 1960s. With shimmering sun on the metal, the shades you have locked into your memory can look totally different.

Racecourse commentaries, as distinct from radio commentaries, started in Ireland in the early 1950s and I have no hesitation in nominating the Phoenix Park as the trickiest of all the Irish tracks for commentary purposes. Before the now defunct Park was modernised in the early 1980s, the commentary box used to be situated above the weighing room area, giving a 'head on' view of most of the action. The horses were either running straight at you, or away from you, in most races.

Only for a few fleeting seconds, as they raced across the top of the course, was it possible to see the horses 'side on'. Identification was always difficult at The Park and anyone who ever called a race there would be a liar if they claimed the 'guessing' factor did not exist.

My son, Tony, once said that it was a pity the Artane Boys Band, who used to trumpet the start of races at the 'old' Park with a short blast on their instruments, didn't do commentators a big favour by completing the tune each time. He had a point. Some commentators use coloured pencils to sketch in the jockeys colours on their racecard. Others rely on their ability to memorise without putting pencil to paper.

When commentating on a regular basis, I was usually content to get the declared runners and run through each race on the night before the meeting. When I found races where the number of easy identifications (horse names = jockey's colours) were outnumbered by previously unraced horses, or animals that had run only once or twice, I got to the track early the following day to concentrate. Always someone who believed in getting to a race meeting, or football or hurling game for that matter, as early as possible, I used to position myself as close as I could to the Clerk of the Scales to watch the jockeys weighing out and to glean titbits from trainers, or members of their staff, as they arrived to declare their horses. This practice served two purposes. It helped cement the different sets of colours (and shades could vary, especially if an owner had bought a new set of silks) in the memory and it also enabled me pick up background information about jockeys, owners or trainers, which helped if one was doing radio or television commentaries on the day in question.

By the nature of the sport, things happen a lot quicker in flat racing than in the jumping game. Consequently, there is a greater emphasis on trying to get things right first time. But hurdle races and steeplechase, while run at a slower pace, present their own problems. Spotting fallers, especially when the field is well spread out, with maybe a couple of fences between the first and last horses, is probably the trickiest aspect. If a commentator always looks back to see whether the stragglers have safely jumped a fence, the chances are he will have missed one of the leaders falling when he turns his binoculars (I always used Zeiss 10×50) back to the front-runners.

A similar problem arises doing television commentaries. The theory is that one should concentrate on the picture on the commentator's monitor (i.e. the same picture which is being transmitted to the viewing public). The theory is fine, but if one concentrates on the monitor then the chances are that fallers, a pile-up of horses or some other incident will be missed, if the monitor is showing only the leaders. For this reason, I was never a monitor man.

For me the National was the 'big one' every year and it was the only race where my commentary preparation usually began weeks before the event. The work began after the weights for the National were published. The routine was to use cards, with the colours pencilled in (different members of the family helped me over the years) on one side and with the horse's name written on the back of each card. I would carry the pack around with me in the weeks leading up to the race, discarding some as horses were withdrawn, and using any spare time I had to shuffle the cards until I was happy I knew them. It was always important to watch out for the late sale of a National runner. It happened quite frequently and there were many occasions when one had to try and wipe a set of colours you had associated with a horse, maybe over a period of years, from the mind and get used to a last minute change of ownership (and colours). I was fortunate to call many great races at home and abroad. But I have no problem being remembered by so many people primarily for Foinavon's Grand National and the chaos at the 23rd fence. Little did I know that a horse, who was only a very ordinary performer when trained by Tom Dreaper for Anne, Duchess of Wesminster, would one day be indelibly linked with a commentary of mine on a never to be forgotten Grand National.

11

Pat, Arkle and Others

Pat Taaffe and I went back a long way. I remember him riding his first winner, a horse called Merry Coon, at a point-to-point at Cabinteely. That was in 1946 when Pat was still at school in Belvedere College. A few months later he had his first winner under Rules at the Phoenix Park. He should have been on the fancied Curragh Chase but this was sold on the morning of the race, so he got a spare ride on Ballincorona which came home at 20 to 1.

Over the next few years as Pat established himself as a top class amateur rider we became close friends and always roomed together whenever we were both on racing business in England. Before he ever rode in the Grand National he would accompany me down to my commentary position and watch the race from there. His big break came at the end of 1949. Tom Dreaper's stable jockey, Eddie Newman, was injured so Pat stepped in for plum rides at the Leopardstown Christmas meeting. He rode four winners over the two days and at that point the stewards insisted that either Pat turned professional or he would have to restrict his riding arrangements.

Tom Dreaper solved the problem by offering him a job that was to last twenty years and turn Pat and Arkle into Irish folk heroes. That famous partnership was still more than a decade away but long before he ever sat on the greatest chaser of my time Pat had become a great favourite with the public. Unusually tall for a jockey, he was a gentle, unassuming soul who loved horses and always gave his all in the saddle.

The Cheltenham National Hunt Festival and Fairyhouse at Easter were the two meetings he most looked forward to and with good reason. He could count four Gold Cups among his 26 Festival winners and no fewer than six Irish Grand National triumphs. The first of these was on

Royal Approach in 1954 and the next year he won the big Fairyhouse prize again on Umm just days after his Aintree success on Quare Times. Happy times indeed!

In May 1955, my wife Molly and I were among the guests at Pat's wedding to Navan girl Molly Lyons and while the happy couple were on honeymoon in New York I had the pleasure of introducing them to the American racing scene in Belmont Park.

A jockey's life is always hazardous and Pat's family and friends were desperately anxious when a few months later he fractured his skull in a horrible fall at Kilbeggan. He was unconscious for five days and it was touch and go whether he would recover. When he was finally on the mend he put it to Tom Dreaper that he might not be able to do his good horses justice and that he should look for someone else. Tom's reply was: 'If you don't ride them, I won't run them,' and that was the end of that argument.

Arkle's early racecourse appearances were unremarkable. In December 1961 he finished third and fourth in bumper races at Mullingar and Leopardstown. He was ridden on both occasions by Mark Hely-Hutchinson who, in later years, could claim with all due modesty to have been the only jockey to have ridden Arkle without winning.

The following month Arkle made a winning debut over hurdles at Navan, an event Taaffe witnessed aboard another Dreaper horse, the mare Kerforo. Pat's mount was neck and neck with another horse at the second last flight when Liam McLoughlin, wearing the yellow jacket and black cap of the Duchess of Westminster, sailed past on the 20-to-1 newcomer. Arkle would never start at that price again, nor would Pat ever opt not to ride him. Together they made racing history, winning in all four hurdle races and 22 out of the 26 chases. The total prize money won by Arkle was £78,821, easily the most netted by a National Hunt horse of his day. Behind these dull statistics there was much drama and wonderful memories. For instance, it is not true, as has been sometimes suggested, that Arkle never fell. He did once, but not in a race. It happened when he was being schooled by Pat at Dan Moore's place at Fairyhouse.

Central to the Arkle story was the rivalry that grew up between 'Himself' and Pat, and the English-trained Mill House and his Irish jockey Willie Robinson. Mill House, winner of the 1963 Cheltenham

Gold Cup, met Arkle for the first time in the Hennessy Gold Cup in November of that year and beat him. Pat was convinced that the result would have been different had Arkle not put his foot in a hole three fences from home. In any event that Newbury race set the scene for the epic duel that was the 1964 Cheltenham Gold Cup. Arkle's victory that day was to be enshrined in song and story, and repeated in each of the next two years, conclusively demonstrating his superiority over his game and classy contemporary.

I have often wondered how many Gold Cups Arkle would have won but for suffering the injury that ended his career. He was only nine years old when he broke a pedal bone in his hoof in the King George VI Chase on 26 December, 1966. Giving away 21 lb, the great-hearted champion was in front as he struggled over the last but was caught close to home and beaten by a length by Dormant. It was the last hurrah for a horse that captured the hearts of Irish people like no other. It is difficult to exaggerate just how good he was at his peak but consider this: in September 1964 the stewards of the Irish National Hunt Steeplechase Committee gave instructions to the Handicapper which in effect created two different handicaps — 'A' Handicap with Arkle and 'B' Handicap without him.

Following his Kempton Park mishap strenuous efforts were made to get Arkle fit again but eventually in October 1968 the Duchess of Westminster announced that, after consultation with the horse's trainer and vet, she had decided the wisest course was to retire him. Arkle lived for another three years before being put down in 1971. By then Pat had hung up his riding boots but not before, at the age of forty, he had once more displayed his masterly brilliant horsemanship by steering Gay Trip to victory at Aintree. In his new career as a trainer Pat enjoyed great successes with Captain Christy, a brilliant if somewhat wayward performer who, on his good days, won the Sweeps Hurdle, the Cheltenham Gold Cup and the King George VI Chase (twice).

Throughout his days as a jockey Pat was always such a calm, relaxed man that one would never have suspected that he would suffer the heart trouble that dogged his last years. A heart transplant did prolong his life for a little while but sadly we are left with just a memory of one of the true gentlemen of the turf, a man I admired enormously and was happy to count among my very best friends.

* * *

The most influential figure in Irish racing in my lifetime was, without question, Joe McGrath. Deeply involved in the fight for Irish freedom and in the first Free State Government in which he served as Minister for Labour and later Minister for Industry and Commerce, he turned his back on politics to become the driving force behind the Irish Hospitals' Sweepstakes. He then used the enormous wealth generated by a myriad of other business interests to establish himself as the leading owner-breeder in the country first by taking over the Brownstown Stud in County Kildare in 1941 and later by resurrecting the magnificent Glencairn training establishment at Sandyford, County Dublin, once owned by Boss Croker of Tamany Hall fame. Croker's 1907 Epsom Derby winner, the famous Orby, is buried there.

The first horse to carry McGrath's 'Green, red seams and cap' to victory in an Irish classic was the peerless Windsor Slipper which he had bought as a yearling. Unbeaten as a two-year-old, and trained by Mick Collins, Windsor Slipper went on to complete the Triple Crown of the Irish Two Thousand Guineas, Derby and St Leger of 1942 in the style of a true champion. Veteran race-goers considered him the best horse they had seen on an Irish race-course, though because of the war it was not possible to try him against the best in England at the time. The record shows that he won the Derby by six lengths in record time at odds of 2/7 and the St Leger by ten lengths at odds of 8/100. McGrath, with his trainer Mick Collins and jockey Morny Wing, formed a triumvirate that dominated Irish racing until Joe's son, Séamus, took charge of the family's horses at Glencairn.

A red-letter day for McGrath senior came in 1951 when a horse he had bred and owned, Arctic Prince, trotted up in the Epsom Derby, thus bringing about an interesting encounter between the man the English tabloids described as 'the ex-gunman' and British royalty. Séamus' brother, Paddy, told me that the Queen (the present Queen Mother) did indeed say that she understood Mr McGrath had partaken of English hospitality on a previous occasion, referring to his sojourn in jail during the Troubles (from which he had in fact escaped).

I also encountered the same nice lady at the races on another occasion. It was in the early 1980s at the Cheltenham Festival. The race-course secretary met me after the second race and told me that the Queen Mother wished to meet me. I laughed and carried on with the job in hand but during the next hour or so four other officials came to me with the same message and eventually it dawned on me that she must have meant it. When I found myself in the parade ring later I presented myself to Her Majesty and found her to be a very sincere and genuine lady.

It transpired that the reason she asked to meet me was that she had heard a commentary I had done for the BBC some years earlier from Downpatrick (the Ulster National) and was impressed. A horse she owned named Laffy had won that race so that had probably fixed it in her mind. We talked for a quarter of an hour and the conversation confirmed what I had heard, that she was a keen and dedicated follower of the sport of kings. She discussed Arkle's breeding and ability and I was left with the impression that she was an 'Arkleite'. She asked particularly after Willie Robinson, who had ridden her horse at Downpatrick, and when I told her he was around I was asked to locate him and introduce him. I was happy to obey the royal command and presented GWR to Her Majesty after the next race, after which we each went our separate ways. When the word got around later I was the subject of some slagging from my more Republican-minded friends for hobnobbing with the Royal Family but in truth I was delighted to have met a very gracious lady. Joe McGrath, I'm sure, felt the same.

It was as a member of the Irish Racing Board and a steward of the Irish Turf Club that Joe McGrath made a lasting impact on the whole racing industry in this country. His forward thinking and ability to get things done helped to bring about such innovations as the photo-finish, starting stalls, course commentaries and the film patrol. But perhaps his boldest move was his decision in the late 1950s to link the Sweepstakes directly to Irish racing.

The vehicle chosen was the Irish Derby, then approaching its centenary but still fairly insignificant in international terms. He proposed, and the powers that be readily agreed, that the race become the Irish Sweeps Derby, in return for an initial sponsorship of £30,000. Thus, at a stroke, it became one of the richest races in Europe, vying in importance with the Epsom, French and Kentucky equivalents. I was in on the story from its conception and Joe McGrath asked me to break it to the racing world at large on BBC television which, of course, I was very happy to do. No effort was spared in promoting the first running of the new-style Derby in 1962, and when the great day dawned a record field of twenty-four including four runners from England and two from France went to post. Larkspur, which Vincent O'Brien had saddled to win the Epsom Derby a month earlier, was naturally made favourite but it was another Irish-trained challenger, Arctic Storm, and a French horse, Tambourine II, which fought out the thrilling finish. A hard one to call but Tambourine got it by the shortest of heads, and a new chapter in Irish racing had begun.

The jockeys involved in that driving finish were the stylish Frenchman Roger Poincelet on Tambourine II and that world-class Australian rider, Bill Williamson, who had come to Ireland in 1960 to ride for the Séamus McGrath stable. 'Weary Willie', as he was known, enjoyed great success on the Glencairn horses for three seasons before moving to England. Some years later he gave me one of my greatest racing thrills when he won at Longchamps on a horse bred, owned and trained by Séamus. That, of course, was Levmoss, hero of the 1969 Prix de l'Arc de Triomphe. In spite of having run several decent races that season Levmoss was quoted at 40 to 1 on the day. Lester Piggott was on Park Top, the short-price favourite in a field of 30. In the race Bill kept Levmoss tucked in behind the front runners, with Lester close by. As they turned the bend into the final straight Bill let Levmoss go and he streaked ahead, holding off the best efforts of Park Top to win. The roar that greeted Bill and Levmoss when they reached the winner's enclosure was reminiscent of the ovation for an Irish Grand National winner at Aintree.

Another memory I have of Longchamps was a particularly nerve-wracking occasion when Peter O'Sullevan and I were both commentating on a race in which four of the runners belonged to the same owner. Over there, instead of the jockeys wearing different coloured caps as is the practice in Ireland and England, the difference is marked by sashes of different colours which, from the commentator's point of view, are not at all easy to distinguish. One of these horses was involved in the finish, and naturally Peter and I both chanced our arm in naming it. Fortunately, we opted for the right one, otherwise it could have been very embarrassing.

I have no doubt that Lester Piggott was the most accomplished jockey I ever saw. His knack of snatching victory was quite amazing. In my mind's eye I can still see him riding his first race in Ireland on a horse called Rise Above at the Phoenix Park. In his never-ending quest for winners Lester would often phone me to pick my brains about the form of Irish horses and trainers' plans so we got to know each other well over the years.

In 1965 after riding Meadow Court to victory in the Irish Sweeps Derby the part owner of the horse, Bing Crosby, led the horse in after the victory to the strains of 'When Irish Eyes are Smiling ...' Many years later I sent a recording of the 1965 race to the Old Groaner and received in return an invitation to visit him in Hollywood next time I was in America. Unfortunately, I was unable to avail of the invitation.

Another rider who impressed me greatly was the American Bill Shoemaker whom I saw 'steal' many a race which seemed lost, and one of my all times favourites among the knights of the saddle is a man who hasn't been seen in a race for over forty years, Martin Molony. Martin, from Kilmallock in County Limerick, was a phenomenon who rode with equal facility on the flat and over jumps and his achievements before he suddenly retired at the age of 26 were quite astonishing. He was champion jockey in Ireland for six consecutive years from 1946 to 1951, having shared it with Aubrey Brabazon in 1946 on the 30-winner mark. His best year was 1950 when he rode 119 winners in Ireland and was second to his brother Tim in the English championship with a further 65 winners! He has no idea himself of the total number of winners he rode but he does remember riding 14 in one period from Saturday to Saturday, including a five-timer at Navan. He was a horseman without compare and a lovely man to boot.

Martin Molony's career was over long before television arrived in Ireland whereas it was thanks to television that Tommy Wade, another great Munster horseman, and his remarkable Connemara pony, Dundrum, became household names in the early sixties. My involvement with show jumping on television had begun before Telefis opened when the Pye Company staged a closed circuit demonstration of TV at the Dublin Horse Show and I was asked by Judge Wylie, who ran the show in those days, to do the commentary. Everyone including myself, recognised that show jumping was one of those sports made for the 'box' — boxing was another — in that all the action could be encompassed in one shot and it soon became one of the most popular things the fledging TV Sports Department did. By a lucky chance in those early years there were no bigger stars than the aforementioned Wade and Dundrum. I well remember the fuss that was kicked up when coverage of the Horse of the Year Show at the White City was terminated on Telefis just as Wade was about to be presented with the King George VI Cup by Queen Elizabeth because someone at the station was under the mistaken impression that British Royalty should not be seen on Irish television. The switchboard was jammed by enraged viewers and later the matter was raised in the Dáil.

That win was one of the many great nights in the life of Tommy and his famous pony, an equine character if ever there was one. Take their record at the RDS alone: Together they won nine civilian championships and two international grand prix there, as well as major classes at Brussels, Amsterdam, Ostend, Wembley, Hickstead and elsewhere. In 1963, the year of their White City triumph, they went through the Dublin Show unbeaten, winning all five classes they jumped in as well as having two clear rounds in the Aga Khan, thus helping Ireland to regain the famous trophy after a lapse of 37 years. That, if I am not mistaken, was the year the Hon. Diana Connolly Carew had to be provided with an Irish passport on the day of the Nations' Cup in order to be eligible to jump for Ireland.

Dundrum was 33 when he died and he is buried on Wade's own land close to the house at Goolds Cross. Tommy says he will go down in the annals as the only horse he ever came across who could win speed classes, puissance, grand prix and nations cup events — and all on the same day if required. There may never be another like him.

There were three grand old men of Irish Racing: Tom Dreaper, Tom Taaffe and Joe Osborne. Of the three Tom Dreaper was undoubtedly the most successful, training Prince Regent and Arkle, two of the greatest steeplechasers of all time, and countless other stars of the jumping game. He trained for some of the big owners of the immediate post Second World War era, among them J.V. Rank and Lord Bicester. Tom ran Prince Regent in England at Wetherby just to find out how good he was and he duly trotted up as a prelude to winning the 1946 Cheltenham Gold Cup. Tom also trained a stunning 10 Irish Grand National winners and his son, Jim, has carried on the good work.

Joe Osborne was another trainer who produced many fine old-style jumpers. One of the best, Coneyburrow, sadly had to be put down after falling at the 28th fence in Royal Tan's Aintree Grand National (1954).

Tom Taaffe, father of Pat, Tos and Bill, achieved something Tom Dreaper, for all his many big race successes on both sides of the Irish Sea, never managed to do — he trained an Aintree Grand National winner, Mr What who won the great race in 1958. Carrying on the family tradition has always been strong in racing. Tom Dreaper, Joe Osborne and Tom Taaffe were all followed into the sport by sons as were many other big names of 'my era' — Vincent O'Brien (David and Charles), Paddy Prendergast (Kevin and 'long' Paddy), John Oxx (John), Charlie Weld (Dermot), Dan Moore (Arthur) and Willie O'Grady (Edward).

Dermot Weld has enjoyed outstanding success, at home and abroad, and is justifiably proud of his achievement of breaking new ground for a European trainer by winning both a Belmont Stakes, the last leg of the American triple crown, with Go And Go and a Melbourne Cup with Vintage Crop.

John Oxx, whose father the late John senior was a good friend — not many people may realise he used to play hurling for Meath, has enjoyed a purple patch in the last few years due to the marvellous international successes of Ridgewood Pearl and Timarida.

But the biggest dynasty in Irish racing is surely the Mullins family. Paddy, a man of few words but outstanding skill, is still going strong down at Goresbridge in Co. Kilkenny and enjoys the distinction of being the only trainer to have won a Champion Hurdle and a Cheltenham Gold Cup with the same horse, Dawn Run.

His sons Willie and Tony are now training while all members of the Mullins family, including Paddy's wife Maureen, have ridden winners. In contrast to all the above racing families Jim Bolger's emergence in the 1970s as a top notch trainer was sudden and remarkable in that he had no background in the game. Now up there with Weld and Oxx as one of the big three of Irish Flat racing, Jim's allegiances, like mine, are often split due to the increase in the number of Sunday race meetings. A keen follower of GAA games, and not only when his native Wexford are involved, he often makes the 'correct' decision and goes to a match instead.

I always will remember Tommy Burns, one of the great characters of the game, as a jockey and trainer and his association with Heron Bridge and Uvira. His son Tommy (or T.P. as he is widely known) went on to become a successful jockey, riding many of Vincent O'Brien's Cheltenham Festival winners and Classic winners on the Flat, including the great Ballymoss. He later worked as assistant to Vincent O'Brien and Dermot Weld and is now playing his part in his son James's training operation on The Curragh.

For many years a lot of Irish trainers fought shy of putting up Irish Flat jockeys when they ran their horses outside the country. In more recent times this policy has changed with Christy Roche and Mick Kinane, and in the last few years John Murtagh, achieving distinction on the international stage. Kinane, son of Tommy, who rode one of my all time favourites, Monksfield, to many of his great successes, has developed into one of the world's best jockeys and is one of the genuine superstars of Irish sport.

And while Mick has reached the top of the tree since my active involvement in the game finished, I get a tremendous kick from viewing his big race successes on TV.

I cannot conclude this gallery of the famous and the great without mentioning the five Uachtaráin na hÉireann that I have met under a variety of circumstances. Seán T. Ó Ceallaigh was a regular attender at the Curragh race meetings and I remember once when he was passing through the weigh room en route to the Presidential box he stopped to have a word with me. We spoke *as Gaelige* and as we parted he gave me a wink, obviously enjoying the fact that in those particular surroundings it was unlikely that anyone present could understand what was being said.

I also associated a conversation in Irish with my memory of Eamon de Valera. I was a patient in the Mater Nursing Home in 1968 when suddenly there was a great flurry of activity. I was told the President was coming to see me. I thought the nurses were joking but a few minutes later a military officer entered the room followed by President de Valera. He sat down on the bed and chatted away, in Irish. I must admit I was surprised that I was able to converse as easily as I did. He told me about King Baudouin of Belgium's visit to Áras an Uachtaráin and of how Jack Lynch, then Taoiseach, had showed him how to use a hurley. Dev himself tried having a puck and was amazed it went so well as he could hardly see the ball. For the record, he told me that hurling was his favourite game, followed by rugby.

I met Patrick Hillery several times during his term in the Park. He is, of course, a very keen and versatile sportsman who knows his No. 8 iron from his hurley. We shared the great delight in Clare's All-Ireland victories in September 1995. Mary Robinson has attended many Croke Park games where we have been introduced. I received a very thoughtful and much-appreciated 'Get Well Soon' card from her one September when a heart attack prevented me from attending the hurling final. I have also visited the Áras at her kind invitation.

I encountered Erskine Childers just before he became President under more trying circumstances: I had gone to America with the GAA All Stars in 1972 and was in my hotel room in New York just about to set off for the West Coast when the phone rang. It was my daughter, Mary, to tell me that Molly had met with a bad accident and I was needed at home. On my about-turn journey back to Ireland I found myself sitting alongside Childers, then Tánaiste in Jack Lynch's government. To this day I remember his great kindness to me in my distressed state.

What had happened was that Molly had attempted to move the car a few feet in the driveway outside our house. It had an automatic gear and as she had sat in and turned the ignition the car suddenly reversed backwards out across Griffith Avenue and crashed into a lamppost on the far side. The door which was open swung violently out and in again smashing Molly's right leg to bits. The doctors did their utmost to repair the damage and for a time we thought they might be able to save the leg but in the end they had no option but to amputate. Poor Molly. What a dreadful, dreadful thing to happen. Only someone who has lost a limb like that can know the awful trauma it induces, the ever-lasting sense of loss. Molly bore this cruel twist of fate with great fortitude but it has to be said life was never the same for her afterwards.

12

There's Life After RTE

The year of Molly's accident was the year I made the big decision to resign my post as Head of Sport in RTE to become manager of Leopardstown Racecourse. It was quite a wrench. The twelve years since the snowy New Year's Eve Teilifís Éireann pictures had filled our screen for the first time had seen the Sports Department grow from the original group of five to a 20-strong team who accounted for some 20 per cent of RTE home production on television as well as a considerable output on radio. That year, 1972, we had undertaken our biggest challenge up to that point, coverage of the Munich Olympics. The two previous Olympiads, in Tokyo (1964) and Mexico (1968), were both well outside the range of the infant RTE's capacity and budget so for those two occasions we had to lean heavily on our BBC friends. We did send a two-man team to Mexico, consisting of Brendan O'Reilly and Eamon O'Connor, a very enthusiastic freelance cameraman from Limerick, and they came up with some excellent Irish-angle pieces to supplement the main coverage.

Next time round we put all our energies and resources into mounting our own version of the Munich Games. In order to avail of the state-of-the-art facilities the Germans had laid on at the various Olympic sites and in the custom-built TV and radio Centres, we dispatched a team of 23 people, eighteen on the television side and five for radio. If this sounds like a lot of people it was a minuscule number compared to organisations like BBC who had 140 personnel there or the American company ABC who had built their own studios and even their own hotel to accommodate their 400-strong team of commentators, reporters, producers, editors, technicians, etc.

Because sporting life in Ireland was going on as usual in the sense that racing and the major GAA championship games continued unabated throughout the duration of the Games I decided I would be more useful at home although I did make a quick trip to Munich in the middle of the second week to cheer on the troops so to speak and was there when the terrorist attack on the Israeli team quarters took place. By a coincidence, Jack Lynch, the then Taoiseach, was also on a visit to Munich and among those accompanying him was Kevin Healy, from the RTE Newsroom. So the story of the terrorist siege in the Olympic Village fell into Kevin's lap and he reported it extensively from our studio in the Olympic Radio Centre.

Shortly after vacating my position as Head of Sport at RTE I was approached by Tommy O'Hara, Sports Editor of the *Sunday Press*, to write a weekly column, an offer I was very happy to accept. My first piece appeared in March, 1973 in the aftermath of a general election and I amused myself and, I hope, my readers by compiling a Gaelic football team made up entirely of politicians which read: Sean Browne (Wexford)... he was chairman of the County Board and I reckoned his bulk would fit him for the job!... full backs: Mick Herbert (Limerick): Mark Clinton (Wicklow) and Sean Flanagan (Mayo): half backs: Jim Tunney (Dublin), John Donnellan (Galway) and John Wilson (Cavan): mid-field: Henry Kenny (Mayo) and Jack Lynch (Cork): half forwards: Paddy Lalor (Laois), Denis Gallagher (Donegal) Brendan Corish (Wexford); full forwards: Bill Loughnane (Clare) Dan Spring (Kerry) and Hugh Gibbons (Offaly). Quite a gallery of GAA greats. In the same column I adverted to what seemed a revolutionary development at the time: four nuns playing in the Ashbourne Camogie Cup.

A few weeks later in the *Sunday Press* I recounted my encounter with one O.J. Simpson. Yes, the very same. 'Orange Juice' as he was known to his myriad fans in those days, had come to the Railway Cup finals at Croke Park and I had the pleasure of working with him. I knew of course he was a huge personality in the States, having made his name first at the University of Southern California and later as a pro with the Buffalo Bills before becoming a television commentator. I have to say I found him a very personable, charming man who showed an intelligent interest in our games. He told me he was most impressed by the fitness of the players he saw that day, and mentioned particularly the place kicking prowess of Sligo's Michael Kearins. But when asked if a kicker of Kearin's accuracy and consistency could operate successfully in the highly-paid American game he pointed out that the trajectory of his place kicks was too slow and that they would he blocked nine times out of ten. Later that year during my annual jaunt to the US I wrote about that other great icon of the grid-iron, Joe Namath, then earning what seemed like a king's ransom, half a million dollars a season, with the New York Jets. This somewhat wayward genius who off the field enjoyed himself, not wisely but too well, I compared to George Best, then on the way out of top-class soccer. It so happened that in the course of my travels I saw Namath play his last game for the Jets and Best his last for Manchester United.

That was the great thing about the column. It gave me the excuse to go to great sporting occasions I might otherwise have missed, greyhound racing in Miami, horse racing under lights at Meadowlands, New Jersey, soccer at Goodison Park, boxing and show jumping at Madison Square Garden. Whatever was on wherever I found myself I went for a look-see. I also used my space in the *Sunday Press* as a platform for expounding my ideas on all sorts of sporting topics. I saw a Movietone News item about the annual Wembley GAA tournament which 'made my blood boil' with its snide remarks about the 'fighting Irish at play' and 'fortunately there were no fatalities' sort of remarks and I rampaged at the Irish Rugby Football Union for refusing to allow their players to accept a Texaco Award! How petty that seems now.

A year or two later Tommy O'Hara suggested I go along to a Rugby international at Lansdowne Road and compare the scene to Croke Park on All-Ireland Final Day. He picked a good one. Under Bill McBride's inspiring captaincy Ireland beat England on that occasion 12-9, with tries from the peerless Mike Gibson and Billy McCombe. The same season I had the pleasure of watching McBride score his only try for Ireland as we beat France 26-6. The controversial GAA Ban was long gone at this stage and we were living in more ecumenical times in Irish sport. I remember being invited to do a commentary at a charity soccer match between the Dublin football team and a Shamrock Rovers selection one evening at the now extinct Glenmalure Park. It was a most enjoyable occasion and it attracted the biggest crowd seen in that ground for many a day.

A year or two before I arrived, Leopardstown Racecourse had been rebuilt on a grand scale, unlike anything previously seen in Ireland. The Racing Board, having bought out the original owners, the Clarke family, very sensibly decided it should become the premier racecourse in the Dublin area. This they did by investing about £1 million in the new stand and ancillary facilities which at the time seemed like an awful lot of money but which has turned out to be a real bargain. What would such a project cost at today's values, I wonder? £20 million? £30 million? maybe even more.

In order to justify putting so many of their eggs into one basket as it were, the Board felt that the facilities at Leopardstown, the bars, restaurants and so on, should be utilised as much as possible outside race days. My problem as manager was that my background in broadcasting and racing had not equipped me to supervise the running of discos, wedding receptions and office parties and other such functions, and it soon became obvious to me that I was not the right man for this particular job so I left with as much dignity as I could muster.

At last the world began to slow down a bit and I was able to draw breath now and again. I still went racing every Saturday, working for Airs and Races on radio or for television if the meeting was on the box and I continued to do GAA commentaries on Sundays but there was more time to devote to the family. Tony by this time was in his early twenties and had followed me into the field of racing journalism. I had never tried to influence him one way or the other but my passion for sport had rubbed off on him from an early age. In fact I can remember him as a toddler pushing toy cars around the floor pretending they were horses going over the jumps at Aintree. Incidentally, when the kids were small one of the annual treats for them (and for me!) was to go to the Adelphi Cinema to see the exciting newsreel coverage of the Grand National. Some years we went two or three times. Later on Tony would accompany me to matches on Sundays and keep the scoring chart for me. Like myself, in the my teenage years, he loved going racing. So it was not surprising that Tony should pick up the knack of race-reading and commentating well enough to make a living at it as I had done for so long.

Mary, our eldest daughter, trained as a teacher and as soon as she qualified went off to work in Kenya where she met her husband, Hans

Bartels, a Dutchman. They now live on the Beara Peninsula in West Cork. Next in the family is Mike who on leaving school went into the freight business and is still working in that field. Peter, like Mary, trained as a teacher but sports journalism was in his blood and soon after leaving college he landed a job as a junior sports reporter with Irish Press Newspapers where he stayed for some years before specialising in racing and setting himself up as a freelance. He now lives in Naas and between them Tony, Mary, Mike and Peter have given Molly and I eleven lovely grandchildren. Ann, our youngest, gave up her job in insurance and worked as a volunteer in children's orphanages in Romania an experience she found very rewarding. She has just returned and is now back studying.

Not long after my leaving Leopardstown the whole family were party to one of the happiest occasions of my life. In 1975, Gay Byrne and *The Late Late Show* team decided to do a programme about me.

It was timed to coincide with my 55th birthday but I was totally in the dark about it. In fact as I said on the show, it was one of the best kept secrets of all time. I was lured to Montrose on the pretext of recording a radio programme with Fred Cogley and was told Gay Byrne was doing an item about Fathers and Sons and wanted me to sit in on his show for a couple of minutes. I was, as they say, 'gob-smacked' when I was ushered into the studio to be faced by a whole roomful of my friends and colleagues from near and far. On the panel Gay had lined up John Schapiro, all the way from Washington, Seán Ó Siocháin, then Árd Stuirthóir of the GAA, television producer Burt Budin and my successor as Head of Sport at RTE, Fred Cogley, and in the audience all sorts of people from the worlds of racing, GAA and broadcasting. Pat Taaffe, Willie Robinson, Liam Ward, John Oxx Sr, and Séamus McGrath were all there, so were the Rackards from Wexford, Nicky, Bobby and Billy, Ollie Walsh from Kilkenny, Joe Keohane from Kerry, Kevin Heffernan, Joe Carr, the golfer, who was at school with me, Bart Bastible of the Sweeps fame, Dermot O'Brien, the entertainer who captained Louth to all-Ireland success in his youth, and Louis Gunning, the racing correspondent for the *Irish Press* and a man I soldiered with for many years. Then during the course of the show, Gay called up a studio in London and there waiting to talk about me were three more good friends, Donal Keenan, captain of Roscommon All-Ireland winning team and later president of the association, Eddie Keher, that wonderful Kilkenny hurler, and Peter O'Sullevan, the BBC's racing commentator *par excellence*. Gay even had the Artane Boys Band on hand and, of course, Molly and the family who had all been in on the secret for weeks but had not breathed a word. It was a very moving and touching occasion for me, coming, as it did, out of the blue, and as Gay remarked it was very nice to hear people say all the things that are usually said about one after one's gone before that day comes, if you follow me. I remember Gay asked me what I thought I'd meant to people over the years and I told him I had picked out a life for myself as a sports commentator before such a career existed and that I had seen myself as a link between the many thousands of people all over the country who couldn't get to the big sporting occasions, particularly the old and the not so well off, and that I had been their representative, as it were. Twenty years on I would put it exactly the same way. Anyway it was all great fun, I remember, and many's the yarn was told of the funny things that happened inside and outside the commentary box.

Louis Gunning, for instance, recalled one occasion at Killarney Races when as, Robbie Burns put it, 'the best laid plans … gang aft a-gley'. It has been an expensive three days for most of us as one 'good thing' after another failed to deliver. When it came to the last race, the 'get-out-stakes', Louis called it, we were given to understand there was consensus among the jockeys that a certain horse would win. As the runners lined up for the start one senior jockey remarked to another: 'Who's the kid over there, I don't remember seeing him ride before?' The answer he got was 'Don't worry, that one doesn't count'. Of course the inevitable happened: the unknown apprentice went off at a lick and the rest of the field never got near him as the outsider won by 20 lengths. Louis said he could still remember me in the commentary bursting out laughing when the winner went by to loud cheers from the line of bookmakers. I did well to see the funny side of it, I dare say, because I was as much a victim as Louis and everyone else who was in on the coup that went wrong.

On the same *Late Late Show* Burt Budin came up with another case of me being thrown slightly in the course of a race commentary. He was directing the outside broadcast at Naas one day and one of the races featured a well known front runner called Out and About. In no time at all Out and About was a fence ahead of the rest of the field which did not bother me unduly but it certainly did Burt. The camera could focus on only one horse while all the other runners were out of shot, very boring for the viewer at home and very frustrating for the TV producer. Eventually Burt's exasperation got the better of him and into my headphones came his American drawl: 'You know, Michael, this horse is making a mockery of my coverage!' I must admit I found it very difficult to suppress a chuckle and, according to Burt, I actually stopped in mid-sentence for about ten seconds.

A sharp, witty New Yorker, Burt had arrived in Telefís Éireann via Little Rock, Arkansas where he had worked as a floor manager in the local TV station and became a key member of the TV Sports Department in the halcyon 1960s. In his large, black-framed spectacles he looked like a lean, cadaverous version of Hal Roach, a man he greatly admired ... 'The best stand-up comedian on your side of the Atlantic,' as he told me. Burt and his wife, Fran, settled down in a house not far from Montrose and soon became the proud parents of twin daughters. He stayed with Telefís longer then most of the TV bods who had been recruited from abroad to help set up the fledging station but by 1969 had moved on to Yorkshire TV in Leeds where he and Fran still live.

Before he left us Burt and I had a little project going on the side that was both profitable and fun. I had been approached in the States by an Irish-American named Pat Leahy who owned a chain of supermarkets and had come up with a novel promotion for them. A customer who spent a certain amount in one of his stores would get a ticket with the number of a horse in a particular race which would be shown on the local TV station: if his or her number came up the customer won a prize. The films were produced by a company called Strategic Merchandising and were an early version of the 'Race Nights' which are organised nowadays in so many clubs as a way of raising money. The 'punters', having viewed a preamble about the runners before each race, place bets as on the Tote which later pays a dividend to those who back the winner while keeping back a proportion of all bets for the fund.

At Pat Leahy's urging Strategic Merchandising came to me with a proposition to film races in Ireland and England for use in his shops. I, in turn, suggested Burt as the director and between us we set the whole thing up. Remember, this was thirty years ago, long before the days of the hand-held video-cam, and so we had to hire film crews and shoot entire meetings on film. It was agreed that we would cover National Hunt racing only and over a period of about 18 months we set up cameras in places like Listowel, Fairyhouse, Punchestown, Lingfield, Sandown Park and even as far afield as Rome. The raw film was dispatched to New York where it was processed and edited and once that was done I would pop over there for 48 hours or so to dub on the commentaries. All in all I would say we must have put together about 16 or 17 of these shows before the well dried up, so to speak. To quote Arthur Daley of *Minder* fame, it was a 'nice little earner' while it lasted.

Leaving RTE and, subsequently, Leopardstown behind meant that for the first time I could enjoy a holiday. The best I ever had was in 1977 when Molly and I went to visit our daughter Mary, her husband and family in Kenya.

We flew to Nairobi and stayed in the Norfolk Hotel for a day before heading to Nakuru, 90 miles north. From there we went to Kisii where we met a cousin of Sean Graham's who ran the hotel in the town. We saw the running track where Kip Keino and many other great athletes had prepared. In Nyabondu we visited a mission set up by Irish nuns and visited their JFK Children's Home. We ended the trip in Kisumu, on the shores of Lake Victoria.

The only element of work involved in the trip was that I was invited to commentate on the races in Ngong, just outside Nairobi. As could be expected there were many strange faces and names to learn but one I had no trouble with was that of Buster Parnell who was in Kenya for the season. He suggested that one of his mounts was a good thing but, strange as it may seem, it got left at the post and Buster was in some trouble for allegedly not trying. Another familiar face was that of Lord Holmpatrick who was a steward there. The most difficult race to commentate on was that confined to local riders, there were some quite unpronounceable names among them.

One day we were in Nairobi and all went our separate ways. As I wandered around I discovered a bookmaker's shop and ventured inside to find the walls covered with details of dog racing in Hackney, this was because horse racing had been called off in Britain due to bad weather. I made myself known to the manager and was invited up to his office for a cup of tea. The experience showed that racing is indeed an international language.

13

Adventures On and Off The Racecourse

On Wednesday, 3 February, 1984, the evening papers carried the story that Shergar, the 1981 Epsom Derby winner, had been 'horsenapped' from the Ballymany Stud on the edge of the Curragh at about 9 o'clock the previous night. A number of men, later agreed at six, drove into the stud yard with a horse box trailer and a van. They were armed and went to the house of the chief stud groom, Jim Fitzgerald, held up his family at gun point and demanded to be brought to Shergar's box. Jim Fitzgerald, naturally, did as commanded, the horse was loaded into the horse box, Fitzgerald was bundled into the van, and they all drove away. After some four hours the van pulled up and 'unloaded' Fitzgerald near Kilcock.

On the evening the papers carried the story, my phone rang and a male voice said: 'You go to Conway's pub in Parnell Street'. Thinking it was some drunk I replied 'I will in my eye ball'. The voice repeated 'You go to Conway's pub opposite the Rotunda and you will be given a message for the owner of Shergar. Do not tell the police.' Before I could say anything else he had hung up.

My immediate reaction was to go but I felt I should tell the Gardaí about it. By way of a phone call to Whitehall Station I told my story and they suggested I should go down to the pub in fifteen minutes. This I did, wondering as I went what kind of fool I was. I found a parking place, went into the crowded bar and stood around looking foolish. Twenty minutes and one 7-Up later I decided to go home, thinking that my 'friend' must have been having a good giggle at my expense and that I would hear no more from him.

At midnight the phone rang. Damien McElroy of the *Irish Independent* told me he had been tipped off that I had got a call about Shergar. I talked him out of using it at that point but the following morning I had a call from the RTE newsroom and from the *Evening Press*, so I decided I better say what had happened. I also rang McElroy to give him clearance to use the story. That started things off. Radio stations, TV stations, the Jimmy Young Show, PM, The World Service, RTE, a radio station in Miami and NBC TV news from USA all phoned looking for interviews on what I thought of the Shergar affair. NBC wanted to do an interview so I hopped over the wall at home in Griffith Avenue into the grounds of All Hallows College with the crew to film a piece. The background was very impressive, waving grass stretching off into the distance, as if I were on my farm!

On the following Saturday, when I came back from the races I had a call from the same person who had phoned on Wednesday. This time I was to go to a pub in Blanchardstown where I would be given word as to where the horse was buried. This time he talked more, telling me he was the driver who had driven the horse-box from Kilcock to Tipperary. He explained how he had transported the now dead horse to a mine in the Silvermines. He wanted a ticket to the US and $2,000. He had been promised $3,000 for the job but the horse had hurt itself and had to be put down, naming a vet, whom I knew, who had done the job. I told him if his demands were to be met I would have to get clearance from the people connected with the horse.

I contacted the Irish Thoroughbred Breeders Association who were offering a reward, not a ransom. On Sunday afternoon I met a member of the Association in the car park of the Green Isle Hotel and in real James Bond manner discussed the options with him. We worked out a coded message which would tell me whether to go ahead or not.

I went to the pub in Blanchardstown as arranged and let myself be seen inside and out and, as I had feared, nothing happened. I was at this stage convinced that it was all a big hoax. It turned out that a plain-clothes Garda attached to Blanchardstown Station happened to be in the pub at the time I was there, which might or might not have explained the lack of contact. This part of the story, or version of it, appeared in the papers the next day... 'O'Hehir in Shergar Drama' or some such splash.

On Monday my 'friend' rang again to abuse me for having had the detective in the pub in Blanchardstown, he even named him. This time he told me his name was Paddy, that he was out on bail for another crime and had to get out of the country. He still wanted the money and

I told him I was in touch with the people involved. He arranged to ring me for news on the following day. He didn't and it seemed as if the matter was at an end. He phoned on Wednesday. I complained that he had not called as arranged but he pleaded that he been on a beef-smuggling expedition and could not get back in time. I told him all had been arranged but nothing would now go ahead until a vet had seen the dead horse. He agreed to phone me again the following day. At this stage there were major doubts about his authenticity because the Gardaí felt they had evidence that the horse had been alive when 'Paddy' had told me that he was dead.

Half an hour later I got a call from the Gardaí in Blanchardstown saying they had taken the man who had spoken to me into custody. He had been overheard making the call in a pub and had been reported by a concerned citizen. My friend turned out to be a phoney and known to the Gardaí. So ended an exciting and hectic episode in a mystery which has still not been solved conclusively. It is generally accepted, though, that the horse had died, either deliberately or accidentally, quite soon after it disappeared.

Many will remember my brush with the law in relation to the Barney Curley 'affair' which almost landed me in trouble. One day I had a phone call from Barney, a well known trainer and gambler whom I had got to know over the years from meeting him at various race meetings. He explained his plan to raffle his house and give the proceeds to various charities. He asked if I would be willing to draw the winning ticket and allow him to use my name in that context. I agreed to this and the raffle continued. Tickets were sold in Ireland, the United Kingdom, France and the US and it was decided to hold the draw in the house itself, a magnificent mansion in Westmeath.

The day before the draw was due to take place the Gardaí raided the house in search of the tickets but did not find any. Barney phoned me to tell me of the police interest and offered me the option of bailing out of our arrangement. However, on his assurance that he had got the necessary clearance from the authorities for the raffle, I decided to stand by my decision. The draw took place as planned, and there were only a few people present, mainly press, as the tickets were brought in and I proceeded with my task. The winners were a publican and three friends and as far as I was concerned that was that. But that was far from being the case. A few weeks later I received a summons to appear in court to answer charges of having been an accessory to an illegal raffle. I later heard from Barney that he had also received such a communication. The day came and I was first in the dock. I told my story and stressed that my only role in the enterprise was that of drawing the ticket. At the end of my evidence the Justice, Mr Tormey, spoke in my favour and dismissed the charge. Then came Barney's turn and he insisted that he had followed all the proper procedures and received permission for his raffle and produced letters etc. to that effect. He was, however, found guilty and received a jail sentence. He did, in fact, not serve any time in prison and could be seen at the races a few days later. I must say that at no stage of the affair was I really worried as I was convinced that I had done nothing illegal.

One other story featuring Barney Curley involved a meeting at Bellewstown in which he had a runner named Yellow Sam about which very little was known. It drifted in the market giving the impression that its prospects were not very good. There was only one telephone at the course which happened to be out of order on that day so there was no communication with the outside world. Just as the horses were at the post some bets were placed with the bookies at the course but it turned out that these were very small compared with those placed elsewhere at the time. The horse, need I add, went on to win in a canter and the bookies had to pay dearly for that out-of-order telephone but there were others it served very well.

For some years I worked for the American NBC network as their European Racing man. My first assignment was a very strange one: a January race meeting in St Moritz run over a snow-covered track. The general idea was that the jockeys were on skis and were pulled over the course by the horses.

The next event on that calendar was the Grand National. I was asked to recommend someone to help with the coverage and I suggested Brough Scott. Early in the week we selected camera positions for the NBC cameras to give interesting footage to add to the normal BBC television coverage. The commentary would be added later.

The film was rushed to London after the race and we followed on by train arriving in London at 10 p.m. We were met by the NBC car and taken to a hotel to go to bed. This may sound very dull for a night in London but there was a reason. The work of putting the sound on the finished film began at 4 a.m. the next day. It took about four hours and then the film was rushed to New York by plane. This became a familiar work pattern over the years and many exciting and nail-biting incidents occurred in the small hours of the morning.

Another first in my life connected to my role with NBC happened during our coverage of the Epsom Derby. Someone came up with the bright idea of using a hot air balloon in which Brough Scott and yours truly would be seeming to look down on the crowds arriving on the Downs. I say 'seeming to look down' because the plan was to record the balloon scene a few days earlier. All that was required was a few shots of Brough and I looking over the edge of the balloon.

We had not reckoned on the enthusiasm of the man in charge of the balloon who was very keen to show how high we could go. I remember looking down to see the NBC crew man, who was supposed to be holding the rope, running along struggling to hang on. Eventually he had to let go and up we soared. Brough and I eventually persuaded the high flier that we were very impressed with his prowess and begged him to get us down. He did, we survived the experience and, just as important, the producers got the shots they needed.

The life of a racing commentator, like that of a jump jockey, has its ups and downs. I still treasure the letter, dated 21 March, 1946, from S. J. Lotbiniere, Director of Outside Broadcasting at the BBC, offering me a fee of fifteen guineas to take part in the Grand National broadcast of that year. The brief I got then and for many years afterwards was to take over from Raymond Glendenning at about Becher's Brook and see the horses round the Canal Turn and over Valentine's.

But in 1952 myself and Glendenning and everyone else in the BBC's Grand National commentary team were stood down because the same Mr de Lotbiniere failed to come to terms with the formidable Mirabel Topham in a long-running saga about the broadcast copyright. In the end, after weeks of wrangling, Mrs Mirabel Topham, chairman and managing director of Topham's Ltd, controllers of the race for more than a century, had forced BBC to buy the commentary supplied by her. It was, I am happy to say, an unmitigated disaster as the newspapers reported the next day. The commentary, mounted by Mrs Topham's team of five amateurs, was marred by pauses, hesitations, contradictions, overlapping of voices and that most unprofessional of phrases 'I can't see very well'. The baffled listeners were told that Teal (the eventual winner) fell at the third fence and ten seconds later that he was leading. Wot No Sun apparently fell at the last, then came in third. Miss Dorothy Paget's Legal Joy was described as 'Dorothy's Joy' and 'Legal Paget'. The gallant (and secretly delighted) Mr Lotbiniere was quoted as saying: 'Considering the difficulties it wasn't too bad' but Mrs Topham did not dare repeat the experiment.

Two recurring themes in the *Sunday Press* were my Australian friend Harry Beitzel's repeated attempts to revive competition between gaelic football and its first cousin, 'footie' or Australian Rules and whether or not the Aintree Grand National would survive. The world's greatest steeplechase went through a great deal of uncertainty in the 1970s after the formidable Mrs Topham let go the reins and allowed Aintree to pass out of her hands. A bearded Liverpudlian property developer named Bill Davies took control for a while but he jacked up the entrance charges so high that race-goers simply stayed away in droves. When he opted out it was reported that ownership had passed to an Irish millionaire, Padge McCrea. All the while the threat of closure hung over the course. Happily, the racing authorities in Britain finally got together and worked out Aintree's long-term future.

This was around the time that tobacco advertising was being banned from racing and from all sporting events in Britain. Aintree was due to have Marlborough and Lucky Strike advertising hoardings and on the night before the race workmen were employed to put them up in the still of the night. Early BBC arrivals saw what had happened and contacted BBC headquarters in London. This led to an ultimatum being issued to the effect that if the hoardings did not come down there would be no broadcast of the race. They were grudgingly taken down, the controversy evaporated and Mr Davies left the following year.

One of the worst moments I can ever remember in racing happened at the Curragh after an Irish Sweeps Derby. The drill was that I would do a post-race interview with the winning jockey and when it turned out to be Yves Saint-Martin I was not too worried, even though my command of French was virtually nil. You see, I had met Saint-Martin several times and engaged him in conversation in his quite good English. He duly allowed himself to be led to the interview point and I launched into my spiel, congratulating him on his success and then putting the question: 'Well, tell us, when did you think you had the race won?' My words were met with a blank, unsmiling stare and then a torrent of French, the gist of which, I gathered, was that he did not speak English. Of course he did, but not on live television, apparently. End of interview.

I got on a lot better with Steve Cauthen, the baby-faced Kentuckian who burst onto the American racing scene in 1976, at the of 17. He had already ridden many hundreds of winners when I saw him in the flesh for the first time, scorching home in the 1977 Washington International on a horse called Johnny D. I described him then as the 'new Lester' and I never had any reason to change my mind. What a nice man too.

The most dramatic running of the Grand National in my experience was in 1967 when only one horse finished the course without accident. As the jockeys were weighing out I spotted one whose colours I did not recognise and went over to ask him what he was riding. The rider was John Buckingham who told me his horse was called Foinavon and that it had little chance. Forty-four horses started that day and 26 were still standing as I took up the commentary for which I am probably best remembered:

> '*Heading now towards Becher's for the second time ... it is Castle Falls, with Prince Fulcopino, Rondetto, Rutherfords along the inside, The Fossa, Northerner, then Kirtle Lad and Greek Scholar together and here they are at Becher's and over Becher's the loose horse is over in front ... he doesn't seem to interfere with any ... Rutherfords lost a bit of ground there but he's all right and they're turning now to the fence after Becher's and as they do the leader is Castle Falls with Rutherfords alongside ... and he's been ... and Rutherfords is being hampered and so is Castle Falls. Rondetto has fallen, Principle has fallen, Kirtle Lad has fallen, Northerner has fallen, The Fossa has fallen, there's a right pile up ... Leedsey has climbed over the fence and left his jockey there and now with all this mayhem Foinavon has gone off on his own ... he's about 50 ... 100 yards in front of everything else ...*'

That was it, 37 of the most exciting seconds of my broadcasting career. But it can go wrong too. The one big black mark against me came two years later in 1969. It was the year the public was allowed inside the course. I saw Highland Wedding duck under the crowd as the horses went by Becher's and said he had fallen. He went on to make a sensational recovery and prove me wrong by winning the race.

* * *

Has there ever been a better trainer than Vincent O'Brien? I doubt it. When it comes to horses the man is a genius with, in the time-honoured phrase, an infinite capacity for taking pains. No detail of a horse's preparation was ever overlooked, whether it was their feed, their aches and pains, their individual idiosyncrasies or whatever was required to get them down to the starting gate in the best shape it was humanly possible to arrange.

The meticulous methods which had yielded an unprecedented run of success at Cheltenham and Aintree stood him in good stead when Vincent decided to concentrate on the flat from 1955 onwards. He had already saddled Chamier to win the 1953 Irish Derby in controversial circumstances — Chamier was beaten a head by the English challenger Premonition but was awarded the race in the Stewards' Room. A few years later Ballymoss and Gladness carried the colours of Ballydoyle's first American patron, John McShane, to a string of important victories in Ireland, England and France but Vincent's heart was set on winning the biggest prize of all, the Epsom Derby, and this he proceeded to do no fewer than six times in the space of 20 years with Larkspur (1962), Sir Ivor (1968), Nijinsky (1980), Roberto (1972), The Minstrel (1977) and Golden Fleece (1982) and each is worth recalling for different reasons.

Larkspur, a son of Derby winner Never Say Die, was bred by Philip Love. Vincent bought him for 12,200 guineas, a record price for a Ballsbridge yearling, in the hope of winning the Derby for his new American client, Raymond Guest. Even though Larkspur won his preparatory race at Leopardstown, the Ballydoyle stable jockey, Pat Glennon, opted to ride the other O'Brien runner, Sebring, at Epsom so Australian Neville Sellwood was engaged for Larkspur. It was arranged that Sellwood would gallop the horse on the Monday week before the race in the presence of the owner but there was consternation that morning when the head lad reported a swelling had come up on a hind leg overnight. The work-out was cancelled and the vet sent for. He thought there was a chance the horse could recover in time but Vincent took the precaution of issuing a press statement that all was not well and that the horse might not run.

After being rested for six days Larkspur was worked again and the vet gave the all clear. On hearing the news, Mr Guest proceeded to have a substantial and optimistic bet which did not go unnoticed but even so Larkspur drifted in the betting on the day. He started a 22-to-1 shot in a field of 26 but whether he would have won in a true-run race is a question nobody can answer. There was a frightful pile-up as the runners approached Tattenham Corner, seven fell and several more were hampered. Larkspur emerged unscathed and sailed home an easy winner.

Vincent's delight turned to anger when he was summoned before the Stewards immediately after the race to explain why money had been laid on his horse after he had announced it as a doubtful runner. His explanation was accepted but ever afterwards he was chary about going public with news of his horses' progress.

By 1968, Raymond Guest was the US Ambassador to Ireland. He had not sent Vincent anything to train since Larkspur but in 1966 he asked 'Bull' Hancock, one of the top breeders in America, to pick out a yearling for him at the Keeneland Sales, costing no more than $60,000 dollars. Hancock duly came up with a good 'un, Sir Ivor, a real bargain at $42,000. The investment paid off in a big way. No sooner had Sir Ivor won his first two-year-old race at the Curragh than Mr Guest backed him to win the Derby eleven months later. The bet was £500 each way at 100 to 1, very nice odds considering Sir Ivor went to post on Derby Day the 5 to 4 on favourite. The only snag was that Mr Guest was not there to see his premonition bear fruit as Lester Piggott unleashed Sir Ivor's devastating burst of speed in the last 100 yards. Duty ordained that the US Ambassador should be in Wexford that day for the official opening of the John Kennedy Memorial Park. Still a wager that had netted him £62,000 to go along with the £58,000 the horse had won in stake money was a considerable consolation. Incidentally, we had a TV monitor installed at the Kennedy Park so that Mr Guest could excuse himself from his public duty for a few moments to watch the race and in fact we were able to conduct an interview with him immediately afterwards.

Vincent is inclined to think that in some ways Sir Ivor was the best horse he ever trained, 'certainly the toughest and with the best temperament.' When pressed he concedes Nijinsky was 'the most brilliant'. Nijinsky's record tends to bear that out. He was unbeaten in his first eleven races, including the English 2,000 Guineas, the English and Irish Derbys, the King George and Queen Elizabeth Stakes and the English St Leger and was beaten a short head in the Prix de l'Arc, after Lester, many felt, had given the horse just too much to do. I remember leaving Longchamp that sad day and catching up with Nijinsky's owner, Charles Englehard, an immensely rich American on whom the Ian Fleming character, Goldfinger, was said to have been modelled. Turning to me this portly figure who had everything the world had to offer, said with tears in his eyes: 'But he was the best horse, wasn't he?' Some horse, indeed. He was picked out by Vincent himself on a stud farm owned by a Canadian tycoon, E. P. Taylor, the first Northern Dancer colt he got his hands on. The price was $84,000, twice what Sir Ivor cost, and by the time Nijinsky was retired to stud at the end of his three-year-old career he was syndicated for $5.5 million!

Roberto, in 1972, was to be the third Derby winner in five years for the O'Brien combination. Like Sir Ivor and Nijinsky before him, Roberto was American bred and owned. Piggott's first choice for that year's Derby was Manitoulin, also trained by Vincent but when he saw Roberto work at Ballydoyle he changed his mind. The trouble was that Bill Williamson had already been booked but that did not stop Lester asking for the ride. It so happened that ten days before the race Williamson took a bad fall at Kempton and was out of action until Derby day itself. Although the doctor passed him fit, Roberto's owner, John Galbreath, decided he would not be up to it and stood him down while promising him the same present as Piggott if the horse won. Williamson, in fact, did ride two winners that day but Piggott, not for the first time, got his way, and drove Roberto to a short head victory over Rheingold. Whether Williamson would have won on him is one of those questions that can never be answered.

In the mid-1970s the first crop of yearlings bought by the syndicate formed by Robert Sangster, Vincent and Vincent's son-in-law, John Magnier, included The Minstrel. Vincent was sweet on this one because he was by Northern Dancer and related on his dam's side to Nijinsky. After a successful two-year-old career The Minstrel started hot favourite for the 2,000 Guineas at Newmarket but was beaten into third place. Following a second defeat in the Irish Guineas, this time by a short head, the syndicate asked themselves if they should run him at Epsom. Piggott answered the question for them: 'If you run him, I'll ride him.' Because The Minstrel was inclined to sweat up before a race, Vincent was afraid the noisy atmosphere at Epsom would upset him so he plugged his ears with cotton wool. John Gosden, then the assistant trainer at Ballydoyle, walked the horse down to the start and took out the cotton wool before he was put in the stalls. The plan worked a treat and under Piggott's strong handling The Minstrel edged home the winner at 5 to 1. He won the Irish Derby much more easily and crowned his career in the King George and Queen Elizabeth Stakes by the shortest of short heads.

There was one more Derby winner to come from Ballydoyle, in 1982. This was Golden Fleece, a horse rated by his trainer alongside Nijinsky and Sir Ivor. Golden Fleece ran only four times, twice at Leopardstown, once at the Curragh and finally at Epsom, and was never extended. His winning time in the Derby was the fastest since the legendary Mahmood and Pat Eddery claimed he was the best horse he ever sat on. He was sent to stud at Coolmore valued at around $25 million. Alas, within two years, Golden Fleece died of cancer, a sad commentary on the ups and downs of racing.

Two years after Golden Fleece had done the trick Vincent came within inches of a seventh Epsom winner. In the most bitter-sweet moment of his long career, he watched his horse, El Gran Señor, being pipped on the line by Secreto, trained by his son David. That was just one more twist in the amazing M.V. O'Brien story which I had been privileged to chronicle, in print and on the airwaves, from its small beginnings at Churchtown, Co. Cork to the splendour of Ballydoyle, probably the finest training establishment in the world.

Things have moved on, Vincent has retired from the limelight and Ballydoyle has passed into the care of his namesake, Aidan O'Brien. This young man was not even on the racing horizon when my commentating career came to an abrupt end in 1985 but his success has been astonishing and he seems well on the way to making as big a name for himself as the original master of Ballydoyle. I can only watch from afar now.

There has been the occasional excursion to the races, though it must be said racecourses were not designed with the wheelchair in mind. A few years after I was stricken, Tony Corcoran, who was then the manager of Leopardstown, had the happy thought of including me in what I think is known as the Hall of Fame. It is on the first floor of the grandstand and has a series of panels devoted to the greats of Irish racing, people like Tom Dreaper, Pat Taaffe, Pat Eddery and famous horses like Levmoss, Larkspur and, of course, Arkle. The centrepiece of mine gives a résumé of my career as a racing commentator. It recalls the very first race I broadcast, the Irish Grand National of 1945, won by Heirloom, and to which I travelled by horse and trap. Also displayed are various mementoes of my racing days, binoculars, race cards, a BBC contract and numerous photos from the family album. I was very touched by the tribute and delighted to be there the day it was unveiled.

More recently I was paid a single honour by another of my friends in the racing world, Finbarr Slattery, a jovial Kerryman with a gift for writing letters and getting things done, who was, among other things, secretary/manager of Killarney Racecourse for many years. In that capacity he always made me and my journalist colleagues extremely welcome whenever we made it to 'Beauty's Home' and I have many happy memories of the races down there on the edge of Loch Lein. In May, 1994 Finbarr and the present Killarney manager Michael Doyle surpassed themselves. They invited me to be guest of honour at their first Sunday meeting which he dubbed 'Michael O'Hehir Day' and what a great day it turned out to be. For one thing, it was blessed with glorious sunshine but it was the people Finbarr had rounded up that made it for me. Molly and the family were all there, with the exception of Peter who was nursing a broken leg at the time, and so were many personalities from the GAA and the racing world, people like the one and only Mick O'Connell, and Con Murphy. Christy Ring's daughter, Mary, was another guest and so were two bigwigs from the Turf Club, Michael Osborne and Alan Lillingston and those two fine jockeys, Charlie Swan and Richard Dunwoody. I enjoyed talking to them all but to none more than my old friend, Peter O'Sullevan, who flew over specially from London. Incidentally, Peter has strong Kerry connections in as much as he was born in Kenmare (where his father, Colonel John Joseph O'Sullivan DSO, served as resident magistrate from 1918–1922).

To start the day off, Peter and I were both given the equivalent of the Freedom of Killarney by Maurice O'Donoghue, chairman of the Urban District Council, and later at a splendid lunch I was presented with a beautiful portrait by Kathleen McKew which shows me, microphone in hand, against a background montage of hurlers, footballers, horses and President Kennedy's cavalcade in Dublin in

1963. The presentation was made by the then Taoiseach, Albert Reynolds, always a great racing man. I was very moved by all the nice things that were said, most of all by Peter O'Sullevan's elegantly expressed tribute to a fellow commentator. No accolade can match that offered by one's peers and Peter was more than generous in his remarks. But then, I have always regarded him as the 'greatest'. As a mutual admiration society we go back a long way!

We used to keep in regular contact and enjoyed some successful ante-post bets on big races, and at nice prices too. I recall him putting me right about Amena, who won The Epsom Oaks in 1950 ridden by Rae Johnstone, a close friend of Peter's. 20/1 about that winner was sweet.

Ten years later I encouraged him to back Another Flash, trained by Paddy Sleator, for the Champion Hurdle. We 'got on' in December, three months before the race was run, at 20/1. The horse and jockey Bobby Beasley, an outstanding rider, did not let us down.

14

And the Memories Linger On ...

With the GAA celebrating the centenary of its foundation in 1984 the year was a very exciting one. I was involved in several activities related to the 100 years celebrations but not directly connected with broadcasting. The games remained the uppermost priority, and there was something special about the Railway Cup finals that year being held in Ennis because Clare was the native county of the founder, Michael Cusack. I'll never forget the unbelievable atmosphere in the revamped Semple Stadium for the Cork-Tipperary Munster final. It was the first meeting of these two great rivals in the final for 14 years and they hadn't clashed in a Thurles final since 1960. Added excitement came from Tipperary's burning desire to win this very special final because of the year that was in it and because here it was being played in the town that likes to be known as the cradle of the GAA. Next there was the extraordinary staging of the All-Ireland final at Semple Stadium against the wishes of many people including, at one period, leading officials of the association. The decider hadn't been held outside Croke Park since 1937 when the building of the old Cusack Stand forced the Tipperary-Kilkenny final to go to Killarney. That was an exhilarating weekend of carnival atmosphere in the town of Thurles and apart from the match I was happy to be a presenter of a very enjoyable programme consisting of *craic* and conversation televised live on the Saturday night from the Premier Hall in Thurles.

Tipperary, of course, didn't win in Munster because Cork's ambitions were greater, but more important they were the more experienced team having been beaten finalists in the previous two All-Irelands. The All-Ireland itself was a big disappointment, but the day went off without a hitch in the organisation of an historic event. From the excellent parking arrangements on the outer rims of the town to the traffic control, shepherding and orderly dispersal of the more than 59,000 spectators the organisation was superb.

It was a triumph in particular for the Tipperary County Board and all the locals associated with it, and in general, for the GAA itself who put so much energy into the whole weekend once the irrevocable decision that the match should go to Thurles was taken.

My family and my circle of close friends were very well aware that I harboured a strong desire that one of that year's All-Ireland finals — the hurling in Thurles or the football at Croke Park: it didn't matter which — would end in a draw. The reason was that a replay would have given me my 100th commentary at an All-Ireland final. But, of course, it wasn't to be and the dream of hitting the 100 mark in this centenary year died with the Cork and Kerry victories. It would have been a magical personal occasion if I had been allowed the opportunity to do that 100th All-Ireland commentary before that special year ended.

You see, from my first All-Ireland final commentary — the Galway-Kerry final of 1938 — I had never missed an All-Ireland final. There were some near misses I must admit: one particular year I had no voice on the Saturday. The doctor who called gave me some pills but never told me what they were when advising me 'to take them about two hours before the game.' He added: 'You'll have your voice for the game, but you won't have it for three or four days after.' That was many years ago and for a long time I tried to find those pills again — just in case. All of this meant that I had broadcast 47 All-Ireland football finals and 46 in hurling by the end of the centenary year, but the total came to 99 when replays were counted in. In my time at the microphone there were six of these — football in 1938, '43, '46, '52 and '72 and hurling in 1959.

Sadly I was never to reach the magic 100 after all. Worst part of it all was that I was so near it: just 23 days separated me from undertaking my 100th at the Offaly-Galway hurling final of 1985. And because of an illness that has incapacitated me I've never had the chance of completing my century since.

Everything was going well during 1985. On radio I had worked on the provincial finals — I remember Cork and Tipperary giving us an eight-goal classic in Pairc Ui Chaoimh, Offaly recovered from the

Thurles disappointment to outhurl Kilkenny in Leinster and the Dubs beat Laois in football on the last Sunday of July. Then early in August we had one of the worst summer's days that I've ever witnessed at a match and Croke Park was turned into a lake of water by incessant rain by the time Galway and Cork lined-out for the All-Ireland hurling semi-final. Offaly and Antrim didn't have quite as bad a time in Armagh but the memory that stays with me from Croke Park was of players manfully playing great hurling through pools of water. Hurling a summer game!

Then I was looking forward to the meeting of Kerry and Monaghan in the first football semi-final a week later, but on the Thursday night I was in Killybegs for a club function and when I got back from Donegal on the Friday afternoon I came through the city to collect a couple of provincial papers, especially one from Monaghan as I hadn't seen their team for some time. I had, as usual, switched to the television commentaries for the All-Ireland semi-finals and I wanted as much background information as I could get on Monaghan before Sunday. When I got home all the family were out — Molly was in Lecanvey – and after my long journey I stretched out on the couch with the papers. The next thing I knew I was on the ground and that's where my son Mike found me when he got home from work.

I was conscious only for a few moments and Mike quickly called an ambulance and I just don't know how long it was before I woke up in the Mater. But by the time I did, the family had arrived at the hospital. Molly had been contacted in Mayo and then an urgent message was given to my eldest daughter Mary who was living in Holland at that time. The stroke has left me severely handicapped and it abruptly destroyed any chance I had of ever reaching that 100th commentary, but it also put an end to my working life. Unfortunately, I've never regained complete mobility and nowadays any matches I see are confined to Croke Park or a Munster football final in Cork or Killarney when I'm visiting Mary and her husband Hans who now live in Eyeries on the Beara peninsula in Co. Cork. At Croke Park I'm usually accommodated low down in the front of the Hogan Stand and I'm grateful to Liam Mulvihill, the director general of the GAA, and the staff at Croke Park for the special arrangements they make for me on the big days.

On one occasion when Clare got back to Croke Park in August 1995 after such a long, long absence I watched their semi-final win over Galway from the other side of the ground. I was a guest in the RTE corporate box at the invitation of the station's director general, Joe Barry. The curious thing is that this was only the second time in my life up to then that I saw a match from that side of the stadium: the only other occasion was when Dublin and Galway met in a National Football League play-off in the late 1950s. That play-off wasn't broadcast so on my 'day off' I dropped into the old Cusack Stand as an ordinary spectator.

Needless to say I was delighted to be there to see Clare's win and I was overjoyed a month later when they had that marvellous victory in the All-Ireland final against Offaly to win the championship after 81 years. There was particular significance in that triumph for me since my father Jim had trained the team that last won the title for Clare. He was in charge of the 1914 team and had trained them at various centres in the county during that championship with three weeks spent in preparation in Lisdoonvarna before the final against Laois. Now, here was Anthony Daly's team bringing back the title and the whole atmosphere that surrounded Clare's win, with the uninhibited celebrations following the Munster final and the All-Ireland final, made it a most memorable summer. Who will ever forget the uproarious scene at Croke Park after the All-Ireland final as they gave vent to their joy? It was a good day to be the son of a Clareman.

Because of that same connection through my father I've always had an affection for Leitrim in football and it was a great pleasure when they made a long-awaited breakthrough in the Connacht championship in 1994. As I mentioned earlier in this story my father had trained Leitrim in 1927, the only previous time the county had won their provincial championship. I must admit that as the years went on that's something I never thought I'd see: an All-Ireland in hurling for Clare and a Connacht football championship for Leitrim. How I would have loved to have been the commentator on both those days.

It was God's will that it wasn't to be. However, I did have 47 years of doing what I loved and what I wanted to do even long before I left school. Broadcasting was my dream and it became my life. I worked in six different decades, that work brought me to every county in this country and to many parts of the world, so I am left with a whole host of great memories. I met all the great stars of the sports I covered and I made great friends. If I ever wondered about how I might have affected people's lives then I got very positive proof that I had made some impact from the massive outpouring of good wishes that came from all over this country and, indeed, all over the world when news of my illness spread in 1985. There were messages from so many people — the young and old, the famous and unknown — and so many I had never ever met made known their concern for my welfare through every form of communication both directly to myself and through my family.

That goodwill has never been more evident than in the huge expression of it when I was introduced to the crowd from the centre of the Croke Park pitch along with the Cavan and Kerry teams of 1947 during the afternoon of the 1987 All-Ireland football final, the 40th anniversary of the Polo Grounds final. It was a very emotional occasion to meet all those players, my friends from that New York final, and some people thought it was insensitive that I was pushed onto the pitch in my wheelchair. When that view was expressed to me I assured people that I wouldn't have missed that opportunity for the world! Another day which meant an awful lot to me came on 14 July, 1991 when Cratloe GAA club's new pitch and facilities were officially opened in Clare. The new ground is called Páirc Mhichíl Uí Eithir in my honour and I was thrilled to be there for the opening.

It is true to say that the best memories are of players. You could call them the raw material of my broadcasts. The exceptional feats of so many of them made commentaries sparkle. I came into broadcasting when some of them were in their prime or just coming onto the national scene. One of those was Mick Mackey. He was a hero of mine; when I was growing up he was one hurler I wanted to see. I was lucky that at the time my father was associated with the Dublin hurling — Dublin and Limerick were great rivals then, so I travelled all over the country to see him. He was strongly built with broad shoulders, a wonderful artist with the ball but a good man to make use of his weight, fairly. Mick could start off 21 yards from his own goal and wind-up 21 yards from his opponents' goal down at the other end of the field, side-stepping — perhaps shouldering — but getting there all the same. He was a great man to rally his team. Having this massive youthful regard for Mackey you can imagine the great thrill it was for me to be the commentator on one of his matches in my earliest years of broadcasting.

You can't mention Mackey without also talking about Ring. Then immediately somebody is bound to ask which of them was the best hurler of all time? Well, in my view it's an insoluble poser and I wouldn't like to divide them. They were completely different in style: Mackey used his weight and he used it fairly, let me emphasise that, whereas Christy Ring danced around, and was probably more nimble; he had a wonderful and baffling sidestep and was truly a hurling artist of rare skill — small, but powerfully strong at the same time.

The problem with mentioning individuals is that you run into trouble by omitting some obvious ones and people who admire them as much as I would have are then hurt. But I couldn't let this opportunity pass without mentioning my regard for Jack Lynch, mainly as a hurler, but of course because of his amazing achievement in winning those six All-Ireland medals in succession. I often thought Jack didn't really get the credit he deserved for that. It was really an extraordinary feat of five hurling medals with the football thrown in the fifth year of the sequence of six. He would tell you himself that he was an infinitely better hurler than a footballer, yet it was something for him to convert, if that's the right word, to football at the highest level in the middle of the hurling run. Of course, I've never bowed to anyone in my admiration for Jack Lynch, the person, the statesman and I was pained when he, in recent years, suffered a similar incapacitation to myself.

When discussion like this came up in our house Molly would tell everyone within earshot that Paddy Kennedy of Kerry was the best footballer she ever saw. And she wouldn't get any argument from me because, in my book, he was one of the greatest of all. One day the late Paddy said something funny to me after Mick O'Connell had established himself in the self-same midfield position for Kerry that Paddy had adorned a generation or two before. 'You know,' he suggested somewhat ruefully, 'I'm delighted O'Connell came along because until he came along they'd all forgotten about Kennedy.' Which, of course, wasn't true: anyone who had marvelled at the graceful high-fielding and perfect kicking, long or short, of the lithe Kennedy couldn't have forgotten the man.

Football has always had outstanding midfielders, but the most noteworthy feature about the sport down the years was the regularity with which Kerry turned out great midfielders. Granted they produced marvellous backs and forwards and goalkeepers, too, but the speciality, if you like, was midfielders. Among those, of course, was the man from Valentia Island, Mick O'Connell. Here was elegance, strength, a safe pair of hands for fielding and equal ability with both feet, and pin-point accuracy with his kicking. But perhaps, the difference between O'Connell and Kennedy was their prowess in lifting their team when it needed it badly. Paddy could always rise Kerry when needed but that didn't always happen with Mick, who in my view never really developed leadership qualities even at the height of his fame. Then there was Jack O'Shea. Now here was someone who could do exactly what I've just mentioned: motivate his team-mates and lift their spirits with encouragement and example. Jacko was physically very strong, had a ceaseless work-rate and was supreme in the era that brought 'all-out' football which saw players operate much more flexibly. How often did we see Jacko, and others, range from the full-back line to the full-forward line while still programmed as a midfielder. He was a rare specimen.

I must also mention one other midfielder — a player I have in the past gone on record as saying I'd loved to have seen him and Jack O'Shea together in the centre of the field. That was the late Tommy Murphy of Laois who was the schoolboy sensation of the late 1930s. In 1937 Tommy, who was a student at Knockbeg College outside Carlow, played on as many as eight teams — three for his school (and that included their senior hurling team), the Leinster colleges' interprovincial side, senior football with the Graiguecullen club and all three grades of football with Laois. He didn't reach his 17th birthday until November that year and what's more if there had been under-21 in those years he would certainly have played in that grade, too. Tommy had a terrific leap into the sky, often caught the ball one-handed and quickly pulled it down onto his shoulder, he had tremendous distribution and was an excellent free-taker. I always had a great smack for Murphy from the day I saw him and all the other great Laois players, including the marvellous Delaney clan, playing in what was only my second commentary match: the semi-final against Kerry in August 1938. That day we were both boys: Tommy still $17^{1}/_{2}$ and I just six months older than him. Amazingly he continued to play football with Laois until the autumn of 1953 but continued with Graiguecullen for another two years.

Two of the most celebrated colleges' stars were Sean Purcell of Galway and the late Iggy Jones of Tyrone. Those two participated in what those of us with long memories still regard as one of the greatest colleges' matches ever played. That was the 1946 All-Ireland final between St Jarlath's (Tuam) and St Patrick's (Armagh) at Croke Park. Purcell was at midfield and was sensational in a mighty battle with Eddie Devlin, who was to become an exceptional player also with Tyrone, but everything in the match was overshadowed, to an extent, by the three goals the will-o'-the-wisp, impishly diminutive Jones scored for Pats. The following year the two schools met again in the final and Sean got his All-Ireland medal, which was the first of every honour in football that he collected in a wonderful career. He was once described as the most complete footballer and that's an assessment I endorse. I think that goalkeeper was about the only position he didn't occupy at some time or other and, of course, one of most celebrated displays of his was at full-back in the 1954 Connacht football semi-final. He wasn't the tallest of midfielders (and that's where he made his big name before becoming a consummate centre half-forward), but he had weight and a powerful pair of hips, so he wasn't easily shaken out of his stance. Those who played with him for club or county would tell you he had one of the shrewdest brains in the game and even when the passage of years saw him put on the pounds he was still light-footed and agile as he proved in the successful 1956 campaign with Galway. Without doubt I would rate Sean the best footballer I've seen — just edging ahead in my estimation of Jack O'Shea.

You are in danger of upsetting the devotees of one sport or the other if you give your preference for hurling over football or the other way round. But I must admit that there is no doubt in my mind, there never has been. I have always preferred hurling: I believe there is no sport in the world like it and I've watched games in different sports all around the world. Hurling is something really special and I believe we must do everything to cherish it as a national heritage. Something must be done about present day football. It's not the game it was by any means and whatever the reason it doesn't give as good value as it used to — and certainly nothing like as good value to the spectator as hurling.

The latter could not be said of some of the great, great teams: take Kerry of the four-in-a-row, for instance, they provided such heart-warming entertainment — and so much heartache for the supporters of the opposition — but even the opponents' fans were struck with admiration for a super side. They were the best of all. With Dublin they provided us with many splendid games. Down and Galway in the 1960s did the same; Kerry, Roscommon and Cavan made the 1940s so exciting and Mayo were a pleasure to watch in the 1950s. In hurling Cork — particularly in the four-in-a-row in the 1940s, again particularly in the 1950s and late 1970s — the great Tipperary sides of the 1960s and any Kilkenny team, but especially their sides all through the 1970s with the super attacking moves of Eddie Keher, Kieran Purcell and Pat Delaney were indeed admirable.

Down the decades Kilkenny were always regarded as the great stylists — they were and still are — but that didn't mean that style and skill were absent in any great quantities from other teams. Kilkenny, of course, had Jimmy Langton, Terry Leahy, Keher and in later years D.J. Carey. Then Cork had Ring, Paddy Barry, Joe Hartnett, Jimmy Barry Murphy who I have been pleased to see made such a successful step into management with their 1995 minors. Cork also had those super defenders Tony O'Shaughnessy, Vince Twomey and Matt Fouhy and who could ever forget the hurling defiance and bravery of one of the most celebrated of all full-backs lines: John Doyle, Michael Maher and Kieran Carey of Tipperary?

Now I'm doing what I was reluctant to get into (as I said halfway through this chapter): list players, but the names come parading past the mind, and the 'lesser' counties produced many of these, too. Antrim, for example, had a genius in hurling and football, Kevin Armstrong, Dublin- produced Mick Daniels and Charlie McMahon in one period and Kevin Matthews, Des Ferguson and Norman Allen (both dual stars) in another and several non-natives, most notably Harry Gray (Laois) and Jim Prior (Tipperary), gave the county loyal service. Now I'll be pilloried for overlooking so many more who should have been mentioned. But to those listed here and to the thousands of hurlers and footballers, horses and jockeys I've watched from the commentary boxes over the years I borrow from Bob Hope and finish by saying to one and all: Thanks for the memories!

Name Index

CIRCULATING STOCK WITH EDUCATIONAL VALUES

BLOCK LOAN

BUNCLODY

ENNISCORTHY

GOREY

MOBILE NORTH

MOBILE SOUTH

NEW ROSS

WEXFORD